My Jesus

CHRISTOPH CARDINAL SCHÖNBORN

My Jesus

Encountering Christ in the Gospel

Translated by
Robert J. Shea

IGNATIUS PRESS   SAN FRANCISCO

Title of the German original:
Mein Jesus: Gedanken zum Evangelium
© 2002 by Molden Verlag GmbH, Vienna

Cover art:
This painting of the crucifixion which hangs
in the diocesan administrative offices
of the Archbishop's Palace in Vienna
was attacked and defaced by the
Hitler Youth who stormed the palace
on October 8, 1938.

Author's photograph:
© KronenZeitung/Martin A. Jöchl

© 2005 by Ignatius Press, San Francisco
All rights reserved
ISBN 978-0-89870-987-2
ISBN 0-89870-987-3
Library of Congress Control Number 2004114957
Printed in the United States of America ∞

Contents

ORDINARY TIME

LENT AND THE EASTER SEASON

FOREWORD

During a conversation some years ago Cardinal Schönborn and I strongly agreed that the vital and dynamic image
of Jesus that is the essence of Christian devotion was dis-
appearing. We felt that the principal cause of this loss,
leading to a complete lack of faith, was the separation of
the "historical Jesus" from the "Christ of faith". These
theories had led more or less to an undermining of the
credibility of the Gospels. I can personally attest to the
fact that many who lost their vocations as priests or religious in the 1970s and 1980s left because they had lost
touch with the reality of Jesus in Scripture, liturgy, and
theology.

In this series of sermons Cardinal Schönborn convinc-
ingly brings home the truth and power of the Gospel image
of Jesus of Nazareth, who is the Son of God. "No man
ever spoke like this man!" (Jn 7:46) is the witness of the
temple guards.

Cardinal Schönborn reminds us that a power, charisma,
and fascination went forth from Jesus. The devout believer
who has studied and prayed with the Gospels has experienced this power. As I read Cardinal Schönborn's own
encounters with Jesus, I went back half a century to my
gripping experience when first reading Romano Guardini's
epilogue in his perennial classic *The Lord*, in which he dis-
misses the distinction between the historical Jesus and the
Christ of faith. He writes that "only one attitude towards
[H]im is justifiable: readiness to hear and to obey."

As we finished our conversation that evening in the episcopal residence, Cardinal Schönborn and I concurred completely with Msgr. Guardini that "criticism of Christ according to human standards is utterly senseless."

In his current series of reflections on the Gospel readings for Sundays and major feast days, Cardinal Schönborn in apparently simple sermons convinces us of the experience of faith in Christ. Anyone willing to try will find this vital experience in the Gospels. Meditate on the thoughts of this book; even if you have lost touch with Jesus the Christ in the endless comings and goings and the often facile assumptions of contemporary criticism, you will find Him again. If you have not lost touch with Christ, you will discover new strength, conviction, and joy in seeing this vital and fresh expression of the reality of your Jesus and mine.

—Father Benedict J. Groeschel, C.F.R.

INTRODUCTION

"No man ever spoke like this man" (Jn 7:46). This is the impression simple people had of Jesus. At that time, when Jesus spoke in Jerusalem to his fellow countrymen, when the authorities wanted to have him arrested, when they sent the court officers to take him prisoner, those officers came back empty-handed. When angrily questioned as to why they had not brought Jesus along with them, those simple people from the masses answered: "No man ever spoke like this man."

Something went forth from Jesus—a power (see Lk 6:19; 8:46), a charisma, a fascination—that caused people to ask in amazement: "What is this? A new teaching full of authority" (see Mk 1:27). Jesus did not speak or teach like the scribes, the specialists of the Bible, but "as one who had authority" (Mk 1:22).

Jesus left nothing written behind. Only once is it reported that he wrote, but then he wrote in the sand, and we do not know what he wrote (see Jn 8:6). His disciples, however, recorded many of his words in writing. They reported on his public work, his miracles and healings, and above all on the dramatic events in Jerusalem, his crucifixion, his death, and their meetings with him, and the moment they found his tomb empty but him living—resurrected, they said.

We know Jesus only through their reports, which we call "Gospels". Are they credible, reliable? Do they not draw a touched-up, sugar-coated, transfigured picture of Jesus? Is the Jesus we encounter in the four Gospels also really that man from Nazareth in Galilee who lived at that time but left behind no reports of his own?

Historical-critical Bible research has been concerned with this question for over two hundred years. Every conceivable method of history has been tried in the effort to extract the historical reality of Jesus from the reports of his followers. In the process, the research, the Gospel criticism, has had a strange time of it: the figure of Jesus has simply proven to be stronger. It is too imposing, too intense, too powerful to let itself be touched up, covered over, falsified. The picture of Jesus shines through all its representations in the Gospels with such intensity that people from all centuries cannot escape the attraction of his figure if they do not close their minds completely.

The question of the historical reliability, of the historical credibility of the Gospels is of course important. While this was frequently called into question in the past, in recent decades there has been a multiplication of voices speaking up with strong arguments for the historical truth of the Gospels.[1] It is very probable that collections of Jesus' words, talks, and parables were already being recorded in writing during his lifetime. One must also not forget how accurately and reliably oral transmission functioned at a time when television and the Internet had not yet crammed full and weakened the memory.

There are, however, two additional reasons that strengthen my conviction that the Gospels quite reliably reflect the figure of Jesus better than any other biographical work of antiquity, for instance, the life histories of the Roman emperors by Suetonius.

---

[1] See, for example, Klaus Berger, *Sind die Berichte des Neuen Testaments wahr? Ein Weg zum Verstehen der Bibel* (Gütersloh, 2002).

In the first place, it is striking that the Gospels report the faults of Jesus' disciples in an unbelievably honest and ruthless manner. A "touched-up" biography of Jesus would certainly show the disciples in the most favorable light possible. The disciples learned from Jesus, however, that truthfulness is a consequence of their Master's love of truth. But they also understood that Jesus came to call and free sinners and that it is therefore essential to recognize one's own faults and sins in order to be redeemed by Jesus. In the following pages we will continually run into this honesty of the apostles. It makes the Gospels credible.

Secondly, it is Jesus himself who also pushes for historical veracity. On their journey with him, it became increasingly clearer to the disciples that there was a special, unique secret about him. From the beginning, those devout Jews who had joined themselves to him suspected and hoped he would be the promised Messiah: the one who would bring the liberation of the people and the final peace. They had to learn with difficulty and pain that Jesus is, indeed, the Messiah, but in a quite different way from what they had imagined. They first comprehended it completely when he appeared to them alive after Easter and they truly believed him to be "the Christ, the Son of the living God" (Mt 16:16). And with that, they understood that everything that Jesus had said and done while living among them had this deep dimension of being the human words and deeds of the Son of God. They therefore collected and handed down all that Jesus did and said exactly and reliably because it really was the activity of God in human gestures and words. In the Gospel, we encounter God in the human word, in human gestures. This is the deeper reason why the simple people in Galilee and Jerusalem said of him: "No man ever spoke like this man."

The following short commentaries on the Sunday and holiday Gospels of the Church year intend nothing different. The Gospel texts take precedence. My comments and thoughts on them are only meant to lead readers to a personal encounter with the word and person of Jesus.

I am daring to call this book *My Jesus*, but not in the sense of a claim to possession, as if I could claim Jesus for my ideas and myself. I understand this title rather in the sense of an invocation, a prayer, a plea to get to know him better, to understand him more deeply, and, above all, to love him more. I am venturing this very personal title in the hope that readers, for their part, will be encouraged to declare Jesus to be their own. Nothing and no one could join us together more strongly!

One more word on the cover image and the illustrations: In the diocesan administrative office of the Archbishop's Palace in Vienna hangs the famous painting of the crucifixion that clearly bears the traces of October 8, 1938. That was when the Hitler Youth stormed and ravaged the palace in revenge for the large Catholic youth demonstration from the previous day. With this it became clear that there could be no compromise between the Catholic Church and National Socialism. Fritz Molden, whom I sincerely thank for the initiative in writing this book, was a contemporary witness of these events. He reports about them in his autobiography.[2] The painting of the cross, pierced through by the Hitler Youth, reminds us that Jesus conquered, not with the sword, not with weapons and force, but with love—love, which does not exclude even the enemy. That is the heart of his Gospel.

---

[2] Fritz Molden, *Fepolinski und Waschlapski auf dem berstenden Stern* (Vienna, 1997), 114–17; see also Viktor Reimann, *Innitzer: Kardinal zwischen Hitler und Rom* (Vienna, 1967), 187–98.

The eight illustrations in this book are witnesses from various epochs of the visual power of the Gospel. Two medieval illuminations illustrate scenes from the life of Jesus. An icon and an image from the Verdun Altar represent the iconographic tradition of the Christian East. Two Caravaggios represent Western realism in the contemplation of Jesus. Finally, two photos of Michelangelo's *Pietà* recall the unique vision of that genius, captured by the photos of my recently deceased friend Robert Hupka, which are unique in their own way. In his artistic vision I have sensed something of the creative power that he drew from the encounter with "his Jesus".

Finally, more words of thanks: to my collaborator Dr. Hubert Philipp Weber, who once again competently looked after the manuscript. To Mr. Erich Leitenberger, Ms. Christine Mitter, and Mr. Andreas Gutenbrunner of the Archdiocese of Vienna, as well as Claus Pandi, Ms. Diana Krulei, and Ms. Susanne Zitter respectively, who, in the editorial staff of the *Kronen Zeitung*, looked after the Gospel commentaries every week, which, after a year, now appear as a book. My sincere thanks, above all, are to Hans Dichand, who invited me to comment in the *Kronen Zeitung* on the Gospel Sunday after Sunday and on the major holidays as well. I accepted this offer, despite much criticism, with joy. What could be more beautiful than to offer the word of the good news to such a great host of readers week after week and to contribute a few suggestions, so that it can truly be the "word of life" that brings God's light and love into the midst of our often arduous and heavily burdened lives? May this concern be served by the volume presented here, which contains the Gospels of the first of the three cycles of readings, the "Matthew" cycle.

Vienna, October 1, 2002
Feast of Saint Thérèse of Lisieux

Advent

and

the Christmas Season

First Sunday of Advent

The Gospel of Matthew 24:29–44

"*Immediately after the tribulation of those days the sun will be darkened, and the moon will not give its light, and the stars will fall from heaven, and the powers of the heavens will be shaken; then will appear the sign of the Son of man in heaven, and then all the tribes of the earth will mourn, and they will see the Son of man coming on the clouds of heaven with power and great glory; and he will send out his angels with a loud trumpet call, and they will gather his elect from the four winds, from one end of heaven to the other.*

"*From the fig tree learn its lesson: as soon as its branch becomes tender and puts forth its leaves, you know that summer is near. So also, when you see all these things, you know that he is near, at the very gates. Truly, I say to you, this generation will not pass away till all these things take place. Heaven and earth will pass away, but my words will not pass away.*

"*But of that day and hour no one knows, not even the angels of heaven, nor the Son, but the Father only. As were the days of Noah, so will be the coming of the Son of man. For as in those days before the flood they were eating and drinking, marrying and giving in marriage, until the day when Noah entered the ark, and they did not know until the flood came and swept them all away, so will be the coming of the Son of man. Then two men will be in the field; one is taken and one is left. Two women will be grinding at the mill; one is taken and one is left. Watch therefore, for you do not know*

21

on what day your Lord is coming. But know this, that if the householder had known in what part of the night the thief was coming, he would have watched and would not have let his house be broken into. Therefore you also must be ready; for the Son of man is coming at an hour you do not expect."

ᆯ

Therefore You Must Be Ready

"Advent" means arrival. Advent is a time of preparation for an arrival. The topic of today's Gospel, however, is not Christmas, the feast of the birth of Jesus Christ, but a different, final arrival: when Christ will come again at the end of time. In Jerusalem, a few days before his death, Jesus speaks of the end time. He calls himself the "Son of man", and he promises that he will come "with great power and glory".

That will then be the "Day of Judgment", the Last Judgment, the "end of the world".

When will that be? Jesus does not announce a time plan. But that "heaven and earth will pass away" is certain. One day, even if it is in a billion years, this universe will come to an end even as it once, a billion years ago, came into being.

And it is certain that everything on earth is transitory, even the mightiest kingdoms, the most beautiful buildings, the most magnificent works. It is also certain that one day our last hour will strike.

Today's Gospel speaks of this "Advent", and Jesus tells us how we are to prepare ourselves for what is coming.

He gives two very clear pieces of advice. Learn from nature. When the branches on the trees become tender and put forth leaves, you know that summer is near. In this way we should also recognize when the end is around the corner. Serious illness or old age tells us that the time to set out, to go home to God, is near. Anyone who does not want to admit this deceives himself.

And Jesus gives a second practical piece of advice. Learn from your own daily life. If you knew when the thief was coming, you would remain alert. Since we do not know this, only one thing helps: Watch, be vigilant! For only watchfulness protects us from unpleasant surprises. Like a thief in the night, so "the Son of man" will come, so our last hour will descend upon us, "at an hour you do not expect". For the thousands who died on September 11, 2001, in the World Trade Center in New York, death came quite unexpectedly; equally so for the many who die on our streets. Hence Jesus' simple call: "Watch therefore, for you do not know on what day your Lord is coming."

It is certain that the last hour is coming; it is uncertain when it is coming. We can drive away the thought of it and live for the day—like the people before the flood. Or we can keep ourselves ready, not in fear and panic, but in anticipation of that day when the times comes that we are allowed to go home to God. With this attitude, we will also see our transitory lives with different eyes. Then *every day* will be precious, a coming of God, an Advent.

Second Sunday of Advent

The Gospel of Matthew 3:1–12

In those days came John the Baptist, preaching in the wilderness of Judea, "Repent, for the kingdom of heaven is at hand." For this is he who was spoken of by the prophet Isaiah when he said,

"The voice of one crying in the wilderness:
Prepare the way of the Lord,
make his paths straight."

Now John wore a garment of camel's hair, and a leather belt around his waist; and his food was locusts and wild honey. Then went out to him Jerusalem and all Judea and all the region about the Jordan, and they were baptized by him in the river Jordan, confessing their sins.

But when he saw many of the Pharisees and Saddu- cees coming for baptism, he said to them, "You brood of vipers! Who warned you to flee from the wrath to come? Bear fruit that befits repentance, and do not presume to say to yourselves, 'We have Abraham as our father'; for I tell you, God is able from these stones to raise up children to Abraham. Even now the axe is laid to the root of the trees; every tree therefore that does not bear good fruit is cut down and thrown into the fire.

"I baptize you with water for repentance, but he who is coming after me is mightier than I, whose sandals I am not worthy to carry; he will baptize you with the Holy Spirit and with fire. His winnowing fork is in his hand, and he will clear his threshing floor and gather his

wheat into the granary, but the chaff he will burn with unquenchable fire."

❧

One Who Pointed the Way

This John, whom the people called the "Baptist", was strict. His call to repentance was hard, relentless. And despite this, the people flocked to him from far away. John was one who did not tell the people what they wanted to hear; perhaps this was exactly what attracted so many to him. I myself experienced Padre Pio (d. 1968) firsthand, the Capuchin from southern Italy who was canonized in 2002. He also hit hard, had serious talks with the countless people who came to him. Even today, seven million people come to his tomb every year. Why? What is the great attraction? Because he was credible! Because everything about him was genuine and because his strictness was not grim fanaticism but came from profound kind-heartedness. And that is why people waited in endless lines before his confessional to unload their burdens to him, to go away liberated and comforted again.

It must have been like that with John. His call to repentance affected hearts. People bought his warning that things were serious, that it was time for rethinking things and repenting, and that it was high time to change their lives. And so tongues were loosed in his presence; people dared to say what was wrong in their lives, to admit that they were guilty and that they regretted it. And in order to make the cleansing of heart and conscience visible as well, John immersed them in the waters of the Jordan.

But when the upper society, the pious and the power-ful, also began to come to him—the Pharisees and the Sadducees—John intensified things even further: "You brood of vipers!" he called them. This also reminds me of Padre Pio. To the mighty, the reputable, he was particularly strict, whether they were priests, bishops, or celebrities of the world. He could be relentless with them, not out of hard-ness of heart, but because they are especially in danger of nurturing a false security, of overestimating themselves, of believing that it is other people, above all, who have to change. It is precisely to them that John the Baptist made it clear: Before God you cannot rely on any privileges, any exalted positions. "Show fruits of repentance!" You, too, and especially you must measure your lives by your "good fruits".

"Prepare the way of the Lord": John was the "forerun-ner" of Jesus, the one who prepared his way. That is why his special place in Advent is that of preparing the arrival of Christ. The Baptist did not place himself in the center. He referred to the one "who is coming after me". This was also what made him so credible and attractive. He did not want to bind people to himself; rather he wanted to open them up to Christ. Whenever he succeeded in this, he was happy, because he lived completely for this.

The Gospel of Matthew 11:2–11

Now when John heard in prison about the deeds of the Christ, he sent word by his disciples and said to him, "Are you he who is to come, or shall we look for another?" And Jesus answered them, "Go and tell John what you hear and see: the blind receive their sight and the lame walk, lepers are cleansed and the deaf hear, and the dead are raised up, and the poor have good news preached to them. And blessed is he who takes no offense at me."

As they went away, Jesus began to speak to the crowds concerning John: "What did you go out into the wilderness to behold? A reed shaken by the wind? Why then did you go out? To see a man dressed in soft robes? Behold, those who wear soft robes are in kings' houses. Why then did you go out? To see a prophet? Yes, I tell you, and more than a prophet. This is he of whom it is written,

'Behold, I send my messenger before your face,

who shall prepare your way before you.'

Truly, I say to you, among those born of women there has arisen no one greater than John the Baptist; yet he who is least in the kingdom of heaven is greater than he."

෧

Who Is the Savior?

The third Sunday of Advent is called *Gaudete*, "rejoice!" Thus begins the Mass today. Many Advent wreaths have for

27

their third candle a pink-colored one as a symbol of joy that Christmas, the coming of Jesus Christ, is near.

In today's Gospel, of course, the joy is not yet in view at first. Rather, we see someone who does not deserve to be in prison. John the Baptist had the courage to admonish Herod directly; it was wrong for Herod to have taken Herodias, the wife of his brother. Herodias hated John for this reason and wanted to take revenge. At her instigation, Herod had him thrown in prison, and in the end she would even ask for his head as well and would get it.

In prison, John undergoes a profound crisis, darkness and doubt, inner night. Was he mistaken? What he is hearing about Jesus does not go with what he has been expecting. He had announced a radical change. God would finally set an end to injustice through the one he sent, the Messiah, and would bring peace and justice on earth. Instead of this, evil is increasing everywhere; he himself has to experience it in his own body, and God is silent; and Jesus, on whom he was setting his hope, seems incapable of bringing about the change. Things are getting worse, not better. In his inner distress, he sends someone to Jesus to ask him directly: Are you the Redeemer—or am I mistaken?

This is a cry for help from a man for whom everything threatens to become meaningless.

It is a comfort to see that even great men like John had to go through the dark times that many, even today, are not spared: when, for instance, a serious illness or an accident thwarts all of life's plans; when experiences of isolation, of loneliness, call into question all of life's meaning. In such times, John is truly a brother in need.

Jesus does not give him a direct answer. "Tell John what you see and hear."

Something is actually happening: The blind see again; the deaf hear; the lame walk! And the gospel is reaching the poor.

This is happening today as well. Time and again people are cured in miraculous ways. At the Marian pilgrimage town of Lourdes alone, fifty-four healings have been acknowledged thus far to be unexplainable, even by doctors. And the gospel really has reached all corners of the world.

And yet the gnawing question that tormented John the Baptist in prison remains: Should we perhaps wait for a different, more successful Messiah and Savior? Many thought this in the twentieth century when they shouted, "*Heil Hitler*", and expected from him the solution to all problems. Even more bitter was the disappointment. Jesus does not promise a salvation that does away with all troubles. "Blessed is he who takes no offense at me." With this, he says: Yes, I am he, the Messiah and Savior, but do not be offended if I seem to be so powerless. Jesus does not save John from prison and death. He does not save himself from the Cross. Nor does he prevent us from encountering trouble and sorrow. But he does give us the power of faith. He shows how great John the Baptist was because he built on God and not on luxury and comfort. And every man who places his faith in Jesus and trusts him, he calls "great in the kingdom of heaven".

FOURTH SUNDAY OF ADVENT

The Gospel of Matthew 1:18–24

*Now the birth of Jesus Christ took place in this way.
When his mother Mary had been betrothed to Joseph,
before they came together she was found to be with child
of the Holy Spirit; and her husband Joseph, being a just
man and unwilling to put her to shame, resolved to send
her away quietly. But as he considered this, behold, an
angel of the Lord appeared to him in a dream, saying,
"Joseph, son of David, do not fear to take Mary your
wife, for that which is conceived in her is of the Holy
Spirit; she will bear a son, and you shall call his name
Jesus, for he will save his people from their sins." All this
took place to fulfil what the Lord had spoken by the prophet:*
   *"Behold, a virgin shall conceive and bear a son,
   and his name shall be called Emmanuel"*
*(which means, God with us). When Joseph woke from
sleep, he did as the angel of the Lord commanded him; he
took his wife.*

               ε

Christmas—No Fairy Tale

It is reported so soberly: Mary is engaged to Joseph. According to Jewish law, the two engaged people are already
regarded as husband and wife, even though they have not

yet lived together. Right before the wedding, Joseph notices that Mary is pregnant. The child is not from him. Has his fiancée been unfaithful? A most serious matter at that time: the punishment for adultery is death by stoning. The pain of the supposed infidelity weighs even greater.

But Joseph does not want to take revenge, which he could easily do if he only makes public that it is not by him that she is pregnant. Joseph does not want to "expose" her. He wants to dismiss her in such a way that no shadow falls on her—quietly. The Gospel says Joseph is "just", which means in biblical language: an upright person, without falseness, without vengeance, who does not bear a grudge; a person who completely looks to and trusts God.

We have an inkling of the kind of battles that take place in Joseph's heart. Because he is such an upright person, he cannot imagine that his fiancée has deceived him. But she is, nevertheless, pregnant. In the midst of these gnawing questions, a dream comes to him. A messenger of God appears to him, an angel, and tells him that the child Mary is expecting is not from another man, but from God's Holy Spirit. And Joseph awakes and trusts and believes the humanly unbelievable. He believes that this child is from God. And he trusts Mary.

Those who believe in the Christmas story do exactly this. The Christ Child is God's Son, who became man. The child to whom Mary gives birth in Bethlehem's stall really is true God and true man, whom the angel calls "Emmanuel", "God with us".

Joseph is therefore the first to believe in Christmas. Joseph is the first to venture the leap in opening himself up to the great mystery of God himself coming to us in this child. And he completely agrees to take in Mary and the child she has conceived and to be a father to him.

What impresses me about Saint Joseph is this readiness to agree to the surprises God sends into his life. Joseph never speaks in the Gospel; without many words, he always simply does what God asks of him.

If we really want to celebrate Christmas as the festival of faith, then it is good to look at Joseph's attitude. With his upright heart, he comprehends what is incomprehensible for human reason alone: that God makes himself so small and can become a human child in order to be there as a man for us men. The name that he is to give the child is "Jesus", which means "God saves". If it were not so, then Christmas would be nothing more than a nice fairy tale.

CHRISTMAS

The Gospel of John 1:1–18

*In the beginning was the Word, and the Word was with
God, and the Word was God.*

*He was in the beginning with God; all things were
made through him, and without him was not anything
made that was made. In him was life, and the life was the
light of men. The light shines in the darkness, and the
darkness has not overcome it.*

*There was a man sent from God, whose name was
John. He came for testimony, to bear witness to the light,
that all might believe through him. He was not the light,
but came to bear witness to the light.*

*The true light that enlightens every man was coming
into the world. He was in the world, and the world was
made through him, yet the world knew him not. He came
to his own home, and his own people received him not.
But to all who received him, who believed in his name, he
gave power to become children of God; who were born,
not of blood nor of the will of the flesh nor of the will of
man, but of God.*

*And the Word became flesh and dwelt among us, full of
grace and truth; we have beheld his glory, glory as of the
only-begotten Son from the Father. (John bore witness to
him, and cried, "This was he of whom I said, 'He who
comes after me ranks before me, for he was before me.' ")
And from his fulness have we all received, grace upon
grace. For the law was given through Moses; grace and
truth came through Jesus Christ. No one has ever seen*

*God; the only-begotten Son, who is in the bosom of the
Father, he has made him known.*

୨ବ

God's Light Has Appeared

The Gospel for Christmas is one of the most solemn texts
of Holy Scripture: the so-called Prologue of John's Gospel. They are words that announce in stately language a
mystery, the original mystery of the world; they are words
illuminating the origin, meaning, and goal of everything.
The middle verse is the reason why this Gospel is read on
the Feast of Christmas. "And the Word became flesh and
dwelt among us."

John, who wrote these words down in his old age, does
not tell about Bethlehem, about the stall, about the shepherds,
about the little child with Mary and Joseph. His eye goes
far back to the first beginnings of the world and enters
deeply into that which is hidden beneath the external events
of Christmas.

"In the beginning was the Word"—so John begins. It is
the same Word that stands at the beginning of the Bible:
"In the beginning God created heaven and earth." "Beginning", as it is used here, means more than the Big Bang
with which—so the scientists say—everything began. "Beginning", as it is used here, means the origin, the original source
from which everything comes. God himself is this origin,
and everything that exists has his mighty creative Word to
thank for its existence: the unimaginable expanses of the
universe, matter, life, we ourselves, the family of mankind.

But God was never alone: his Word was always with him, "the only one who is God and who is in the bosom of the Father", John says in his hymn-like language. Through the Word, the Son, God created everything. That is also why the Word of God is very near to every person. John says that this is "the light that enlightens every man". In the heart of every person there is this light, this spark of light, that always lights up when we understand something, when something "en-lightens" us.

Christ is this light—the light that has always enlightened every person who sincerely seeks the true and the good. Many people do not yet know where this light in their life comes from. The source of the light is still not known to them. The light also meets with the resistance of darkness. Light and darkness are engaged in battle and have been at all times and in the heart of every person.

The battle between light and darkness, however, was not to remain a draw. That is why God sent his light, his Word, into the world, so that he would become a man among us men: "And the Word became flesh."

"Flesh" is a Jewish biblical expression for "man". God's Word, his eternal Son, became a "man of flesh and blood": the little child in the stall of Bethlehem. For this reason, many artists portray him in such a way that all light radiates from him. God's original light shines for us in Jesus.

This Gospel is unique. Only gradually does it open up to our understanding, over the years, and it is always new and surprising. I advise reading it aloud occasionally. Then it makes an even greater impression.

The Gospel of Matthew 2:13–15, 19–23

Now when they had departed, behold, an angel of the Lord appeared to Joseph in a dream and said, "Rise, take the child and his mother, and flee to Egypt, and remain there till I tell you; for Herod is about to search for the child, to destroy him." And he rose and took the child and his mother by night, and departed to Egypt, and remained there until the death of Herod. This was to fulfil what the Lord had spoken by the prophet, "Out of Egypt have I called my son." . . .

But when Herod died, behold, an angel of the Lord appeared in a dream to Joseph in Egypt, saying, "Rise, take the child and his mother, and go to the land of Israel, for those who sought the child's life are dead." And he rose and took the child and his mother, and went to the land of Israel. But when he heard that Archelaus reigned over Judea in place of his father Herod, he was afraid to go there, and being warned in a dream he withdrew to the district of Galilee. And he went and dwelt in a city called Nazareth, that what was spoken by the prophets might be fulfilled, "He shall be called a Nazarene."

Herod or Joseph

The Sunday after Christmas is also called the "Feast of the Holy Family". It is about these three: Joseph, the child, and his mother. And how they fare is what they have in common with millions of people in our day. How many in this country have experienced expulsion from our homelands, have had to get up in the night and flee to save their very lives! Every day we hear about the massive streams of refugees from Afghanistan, the Congo, Sudan, to name only a few countries, and again and again mothers with children, with their paltry possessions, unprotected and defenseless.

This little family in flight has a peculiarity: the child that Joseph wants to bring with his mother to safety is the Son of God and—as the astrologers call him—"the newborn King of the Jews". They have to flee from Herod the Great, the mighty and brutal king, whose colossal buildings you still encounter everywhere you go in the Holy Land today—not least among them the giant stone blocks of the "Wailing Wall", the western wall of Herod's Temple in Jerusalem.

An unequal fight: the power-obsessed Herod, who smothers all resistance in blood, and this poor little family, whose child Herod seeks to kill. The only enemy Herod cannot have killed is his own death, which day by day moves closer, which relentlessly seeks to take his life and will one day take it from him and, with it, all his might and splendor. Out of fear of this enemy, his own inescapable death, he seeks to kill this child, who could compete with him for the throne. Hence his panic, which even drives him on to the murder of all male children of the child's age around Bethlehem, even as he later will have his own son murdered out of fear of his rivalry.

What appears so crass in Herod lies more or less hidden in every human heart: Just do not think about the fact that we have to go some day—live as if everything were in our power!

Joseph shows a different way. And whoever goes this way need neither fear nor drive away death. Joseph has placed himself and his little family under the guiding hand of God. He has accepted the child who came, not from himself, but from God, not as a possession at his disposal, but as a responsibility entrusted to him by God. His whole life is now focused on this mission. His own self-realization is not his purpose in life; rather, it is his service to this child, who is one day to be the Redeemer of all men.

Joseph lets himself be led by God, but God always shows him only the next step, and this step Joseph must then take himself, bravely, wisely, resolutely. So he flees, he turns back with the child and his mother; he settles down finally in small, insignificant Nazareth.

To let God lead your heart as Joseph does demands letting go of your own will and consenting to God's guidance. This calls for trusting that God is leading us on good paths even if they are difficult. The end will confirm this for us. Saint Joseph is the patron saint of a good death. Whoever lives this way does not need to fear death, because he has placed his life in God's hands. We have to choose between the two ways: Herod or Joseph.

Solemnity of Mary the Mother of God

The Gospel of Luke 2:16–21

And they went with haste, and found Mary and Joseph, and the baby lying in a manger. And when they saw it they made known the saying which had been told them concerning this child; and all who heard it wondered at what the shepherds told them. But Mary kept all these things, pondering them in her heart. And the shepherds returned, glorifying and praising God for all they had heard and seen, as it had been told them.

And at the end of eight days, when he was circumcised, he was called Jesus, the name given by the angel before he was conceived in the womb.

❧

Astonishment in Bethlehem

On the morning of this first of January, the Gospel leads us yet again back to the manger. It wants us to live through the joy of Christmas once again. There are festivals in our time that are intoxicating in their spectacle; sometimes there are festivals that are just plain intoxicating. New Year's Eve may have been such a celebration. The joy of the shepherds was of a different, quieter kind. Whoever wants to share in the joy of this festival must again learn astonishment: the

39

astonishment of the shepherds and the others to whom the shepherds described their experiences.

What did those shepherds near the manger tell? That a tremendous promise had been communicated to them: "To you is born this day in the city of David a Savior, who is Christ the Lord." One must hear these words, so to speak, with Jewish ears in order to appreciate their implications. For generations, Israel had lived in the hope that God would one day send the Messiah, who would do away with all injustice and free them from all disaster. Some day everything will turn out all right. Some day God will wipe away all tears. Some day the poor will be able to breathe a sigh of relief, because God himself will take the yoke of oppression from their shoulders.

Anyone who hears these things in the message of the angels to the shepherds in the field near Bethlehem understands what joy this message unleashed. Today, the old dream, the great hope shall come true: The Messiah, the Savior is here.

The sign given to the shepherds is admittedly surprising: "You will find a baby wrapped in swaddling cloths and lying in a manger." There were countless children of poor people back then—like today. What could be so exceptional about such a sign? Does a mighty savior look like this child, lying pitifully in a feeding trough for his bed?

The astonishing thing is that the shepherds, who themselves were to be counted among the poor, took no offense at this. They found the child in the stall with Mary and Joseph, and they believed what they had been told about the child. They were not deterred by the poverty of this birth. They trusted that God could work in such a small, inconspicuous way, not with great pomp and dazzling spectacle, but quite simply and in obscurity. Only he who has the attitude of the shepherds will discover God's activity in his own life and will realize with joy that God shows himself precisely in the small things of daily life. We are told that Mary kept all these things and pondered them in her heart. We are not told that she discussed them everywhere. Her attitude was different. She examined the events with her heart, kept them in her memory, without many words. She was amazed at the report of the shepherds, which brought her unexpected confirmation of the things promised to her about her child. She would be able to use this sign from God in all the years lying before her, when it seemed that none of the things that had been told about this child were fulfilled in the long thirty years in which Jesus grew up and led the life of a completely inconspicuous Jewish manual laborer in Nazareth.

Two great examples: the shepherds, in their simple attitude of belief, and Mary, who pondered everything in her heart. Whoever practices these attitudes will detect traces of God even in their most ordinary daily life. Perhaps it is given to us once to meet such people like the shepherds of Bethlehem, who, through their sincere trust in God, astonish us and help us along.

Epiphany of the Lord

————

The Gospel of Matthew 2:1–12

Now when Jesus was born in Bethlehem of Judea in the days of Herod the king, behold, Wise Men from the East came to Jerusalem, saying, "Where is he who has been born king of the Jews? For we have seen his star in the East, and have come to worship him." When Herod the king heard this, he was troubled, and all Jerusalem with him; and assembling all the chief priests and scribes of the people, he inquired of them where the Christ was to be born. They told him, "In Bethlehem of Judea; for so it is written by the prophet:

'And you, O Bethlehem, in the land of Judah,
are by no means least among the rulers of Judah;
for from you shall come a ruler
who will govern my people Israel.' "

Then Herod summoned the Wise Men secretly and ascertained from them what time the star appeared; and he sent them to Bethlehem, saying, "Go and search diligently for the child, and when you have found him bring me word, that I too may come and worship him." When they had heard the king they went their way; and behold, the star which they had seen in the East went before them, till it came to rest over the place where the child was. When they saw the star, they rejoiced exceedingly with great joy; and going into the house they saw the child with Mary his mother, and they fell down and worshiped him. Then, opening their treasures, they offered him gifts, gold and frankincense and myrrh. And being warned in a

42

*dream not to return to Herod, they departed to their own
country by another way.*

❧

The Star of Bethlehem

In the vernacular, today's feast is still called that of the "Three
Kings".

The Church calls it the "Feast of the Appearance of the
Lord" (Epiphany) because it celebrates the encounter of the
"heathen" with the light of God's revelation.

First, a historical comment. We have an Austrian astron-
omer to thank for the most thorough study to date on the
"Star of Bethlehem". Professor Konradin Ferrari d'Occhieppo,
a member of the Austrian Academy of Sciences, in decades
of work, researched everything there was to find about the
"astrologers from the East" and the appearance of the star. In
the process, he reached convincing conclusions. In the year
7 B.C., there was a long-lasting, very rare alignment of the plan-
ets Jupiter and Saturn. Babylonian astronomy was of out-
standing quality and precision. Professor Ferrari, who was chair
of the Institute for Theoretical Astronomy at the University
of Vienna from 1955 to 1978, was able to prove that the report
in Matthew's Gospel is reliable and credible in all its details.[1]
That Jesus was actually born earlier than the year zero has been
known for a long time, because the early medieval calculation of his date of birth, on which our calendar is based, was
incorrect. Today, the date of his birth considered most likely

[1] He offered the most comprehensive description of his findings in his
book *Der Stern von Bethlehem in astronomischer Sicht: Legende oder Tatsache?* (1999).

43

was, according to tradition, exactly January 6 in the winter of the year 7 B.C.

But back to the deeper meaning of the journey of the astrologers. God speaks to man not only through the Bible, the word of his revelation—he first speaks through "the book of nature". It is not coincidental that the great scientists were often devout. To this group belonged the scholars from the East, probably from Babylon.

But is it not superstition to believe that the stars can give "information" about human life? Is astrology not rejected in the Bible? The "astrologers" assumed according to the astonishingly accurate knowledge of their time that the rare planet alignment had to point to a special event in the Jewish nation, for instance, to the birth of a very special king. In Jerusalem, however, they were referred to the prophecies of the Bible according to which the Messiah, the Redeemer, was supposed to be born in Bethlehem. Both things, nature and the Bible, showed them the way to God. And so they reached the infant Jesus, fell down before him and paid homage to him. They did not worship the star; they worshipped the one to whom the star pointed.

Thus, they are for all later generations guides to Christ. Our fate does not hang on the stars, because the stars and everything in the entire universe point ultimately to the Creator, in whose good hand our lives are. The simple shepherds and the learned Wise Men from the Orient guide us to the place where we find God in the small child of Bethlehem, who has come so near to us men.

BAPTISM OF THE LORD

The Gospel of Matthew 3:13–17

Then Jesus came from Galilee to the Jordan to John, to be baptized by him. John would have prevented him, saying, "I need to be baptized by you, and do you come to me?" But Jesus answered him, "Let it be so now; for thus it is fitting for us to fulfil all righteousness." Then he consented. And when Jesus was baptized, he went up immediately from the water, and behold, the heavens were opened and he saw the Spirit of God descending like a dove, and alighting on him; and behold, a voice from heaven, saying, "This is my beloved Son, with whom I am well pleased."

ह

In Our Midst

For me, the Christmas season always ends too suddenly. Hardly is the feast past, and already everything is cleared away. For the Church, the cycle of Christmas feasts also closes today with the Feast of the Baptism of the Lord. In the past, the crèche was left out much longer, until the second of February, which is called "Candlemas". Forty days after Jesus' birth, according to Jewish regulations, Mary offered in the Temple in Jerusalem the sacrifice for her purification. At the same time, so to speak, she also "gave back" her firstborn son to God. That is why the feast on February 2 is also called the "Presentation (that is, the Offering) of the Lord".

Why of all days, though, does the Christmas season end for the Church with Jesus' baptism, which he did not request from John until he was thirty years old? What did this event have to do with the birth of Jesus?

Today most children of Christian parents are already baptized soon after birth, according to a custom that reaches back to the earliest time of Christianity. It was different at the time when John the Baptist made his call to repentance. Many followed his call and went down to him to the Jordan in order to confess their sins and to be submerged in the Jordan for the forgiveness of their sins. Luke the Evangelist gives a vivid account of all who came there to receive the baptism of repentance: soldiers, prostitutes, tax collectors, people of all occupational strata. And then suddenly in their midst, Jesus! John shrinks back: What are you doing in such company? After all, you have no need of repentance! I need baptism, not you, John protests.

Nevertheless, Jesus insists on receiving baptism in the midst of this assorted, sinful crowd of people. It is God's will that he do it in this manner.

What moves him to take this step? Why does he leave Nazareth, his family, his occupation? For thirty years he has lived a completely inconspicuous life as a manual laborer. Now he sets out on his own.

And his first step is to go to John in the midst of the penitents. His first official act is something like his "life agenda". Right from the beginning Jesus takes up the place that expresses the mission of his life: in the midst of us poor sinners, as if he were one of us. Even his name expresses this mission: Jeshua, Jesus, in Hebrew means "God saves".

The angel had explained to Joseph in a dream that this was the reason for calling the child that Mary was expecting Jesus: "For he will save his people from their sins."

So this connects Jesus' birth with his baptism: that he came to free us from our sins. That is why he, the Son of God, became man; that is why he comes to the Jordan, in order to place himself in the midst of us sinners and to take our burden of guilt and error upon himself. He does not look contemptuously at the people around him who have come to John; rather, he takes their side. And God straight-away adds his approval: "This is my beloved Son."

Christmas has not been celebrated in vain if we grasp this and comprehend it with our hearts: that God loves us all as his children and that it was for this reason that he sent his Son as the Son of man to the lost, so that they could again find the way back into the house where he is Father, so that he could again say to each of us: You, too, are my beloved child!

Ordinary Time

Second Sunday in Ordinary Time

The Gospel of John 1:29–34

The next day [John] saw Jesus coming toward him, and said, "Behold, the Lamb of God, who takes away the sin of the world! This is he of whom I said, 'After me comes a man who ranks before me, for he was before me.' I myself did not know him; but for this I came baptizing with water, that he might be revealed to Israel." And John bore witness, "I saw the Spirit descend as a dove from heaven and remain on him. I myself did not know him; but he who sent me to baptize with water said to me, 'He on whom you see the Spirit descend and remain, this is he who baptizes with the Holy Spirit.' And I have seen and have borne witness that this is the Son of God."

Mozart and the Lamb

One of W. A. Mozart's most beautiful and moving musical pieces is the "Agnus Dei" from the *Coronation Mass*.

Many years ago, when Herbert von Karajan directed the *Coronation Mass* in Saint Peter's Cathedral in Rome, tears ran down his face during this piece. Why exactly did Mozart compose the "Agnus Dei" ("Lamb of God, you take away the sins of the world, have mercy on us, grant us peace") with such particular depth and fervor?

We know from Mozart himself that he attached the greatest importance to these words and what they mean. Perhaps after today's Gospel we will understand a little better why. For here, in the mouth of John the Baptist, those words, which have become a foundational part of Christian speech, are uttered for the first time: "Behold the Lamb of God, who takes away the sins of the world!" In the Holy Mass, these words are found several times: in particular before Communion, when the priest elevates the Host, the bread that has become the Body of Christ.

Even though these words may be heard often, we must admit they have become quite foreign to us.

We certainly know how a lamb looks. Sheep breeding is found more frequently again in our land today. But what does it mean, this description that the Baptist at the Jordan uses to refer to the strong young man, the carpenter from Nazareth, who comes to him?

Now John does not simply call him a lamb in the same way we address a somewhat timid and naïve person in mild derision. He calls Jesus "Lamb of God", and with that he touches upon a very familiar reality of those days.

Every day lambs were offered as sacrifices in the Temple in Jerusalem, and to this day a lamb is eaten at the meal on the Jewish Easter night (the Seder on Passover), which recalls the night of the Exodus from slavery in Egypt.

"Lamb of God": this means the sacrifice that is offered to God for reconciliation and liberation.

This strong man in his best years (he is around thirty at that time) John calls "Lamb of God". And he says of him: He will take away the "sins of the world".

These mysterious words about Jesus predict his entire future path. He will travel this path, not with great military conquests or with tremendous political success, but rather "like a lamb that is led to the slaughter" (as it is written by the prophet Isaiah 53:7). But exactly in this way, in this seeming impotence, "like a lamb", he will lift off its hinges the entire burden of evil that weighs heavily on the world. For behind all the destructive powers, injustice, war, and hate stands a reality that the Bible calls "sin", and it is this enormous burden, which Jesus loaded upon himself and "took away".

What that really means we will never understand with our brains alone, but our hearts sense it. Mozart understood it with his heart, and in his blessed music he expressed how comforting this certainty about the victorious Lamb of God is.

The Gospel of Matthew 4:12–23

Now when he heard that John had been arrested, he withdrew into Galilee; and leaving Nazareth he went and dwelt in Caperna-um by the sea, in the territory of Zebulun and Naphtali, that what was spoken by the prophet Isaiah might be fulfilled:

"The land of Zebulun and the land of Naphtali,
toward the sea, across the Jordan,
Galilee of the Gentiles—
the people who sat in darkness
have seen a great light,
and for those who sat in the region and shadow of death
light has dawned."

From that time Jesus began to preach, saying, "Repent, for the kingdom of heaven is at hand."

As he walked by the Sea of Galilee, he saw two brothers, Simon who is called Peter and Andrew his brother, casting a net into the sea; for they were fishermen. And he said to them, "Follow me, and I will make you fishers of men." Immediately they left their nets and followed him. And going on from there he saw two other brothers, James the son of Zebedee and John his brother, in the boat with Zebedee their father, mending their nets, and he called them. Immediately they left the boat and their father, and followed him.

And he went about all Galilee, teaching in their synagogues and preaching the gospel of the kingdom and healing every disease and every infirmity among the people.

So It Began

Even the first sentence about the public activity of Jesus makes clear the circumstances surrounding it: Jesus hears that "someone"—that is to say, Herod Antipas—has had John the Baptist thrown into prison. So he decides to move away from his hometown of Nazareth, where he has lived for thirty years. With that, it is clear: Jesus' path also stands under the sign of contradiction. "Someone" will also persecute him. At the end of his journey, there waits, not only prison, but also crucifixion. Why it has come to this will become immediately clear. First, however, it all begins very promisingly.

Jesus moves to Capernaum. He leaves his remote home village. He will not have had much to take along, and hardly anyone will have taken notice of it. But Matthew the Evangelist, who by occupation was a customs and tax official and whose customs office was located there close to Capernaum on the great trade route, which, coming from Asia, led to the Mediterranean—the famous *via maris*, which was bustling with traffic—this Matthew, whom Jesus then called away from his customs office to himself, sees in looking back on Jesus' move that something great took place there: "The people who sat in darkness have seen a great light, and for those who sat in the region and shadow of death light has dawned" (cf. Is 9:2). He knows what he is talking about. He knows how radically the encounter with Jesus changed his life. At that time, light really came into the darkness of his life.

What Matthew experienced, and countless others since then and to this day, is expressed by this one, first short utterance of Jesus: "Repent!" For Matthew, this meant giving up his occupation and changing his life completely. He became one of those who moved about with Jesus and whom he then made his "apostles", those he sent. It was also like this for the first four, the two pairs of brothers, who were fishermen and who left everything to be on the way with Jesus wherever he went.

"Repent!" This did not apply only to those whom Jesus called to be apostles, or only to those who to this day follow Jesus in the vocation of the priesthood or as members of orders. It is, so to speak, the "permanent commission of Jesus" for all times. And it applies for life.

For "repenting" means "rethinking"—reflecting, recognizing what should become different in one's own life, where it is necessary to break off, to overcome old well-worn (bad) habits. "To convert" means to begin every day anew with God.

In this way we learn that the "kingdom of God" is near; that it does not first begin over there, on the other side, but that it is already here now, so that I can already venture a step of "repentance" today; and that following Jesus, going with him, brings light into life.

Fourth Sunday in Ordinary Time

The Gospel of Matthew 5:1–12a

Seeing the crowds, he went up on the mountain, and when he sat down his disciples came to him. And he opened his mouth and taught them, saying:

"Blessed are the poor in spirit, for theirs is the kingdom of heaven.

"Blessed are those who mourn, for they shall be comforted.

"Blessed are the meek, for they shall inherit the earth.

"Blessed are those who hunger and thirst for righteousness, for they shall be satisfied.

"Blessed are the merciful, for they shall obtain mercy.

"Blessed are the pure in heart, for they shall see God.

"Blessed are the peacemakers, for they shall be called sons of God.

"Blessed are those who are persecuted for righteousness' sake, for theirs is the kingdom of heaven.

"Blessed are you when men revile you and persecute you and utter all kinds of evil against you falsely on my account. Rejoice and be glad, for your reward is great in heaven."

❧

Happy, but Not Simple

Anyone who has been to Galilee will never forget what a wonderful view presents itself when one stands on the "Mount of the Beatitudes".

57

There, on this hill over the Sea of Gennesaret, Jesus, according to ancient tradition, is supposed to have delivered the so-called "Sermon on the Mount", its centerpiece being the Beatitudes, today's Sunday Gospel.

The landscape there almost forms a natural amphitheater. Thus, Jesus is able to speak loudly and clearly to a great crowd of people. What he says there is, of course, most unusual.

Jesus calls men "blessed", that is, happy, who live in situations that we naturally cannot help but regard as not at all pleasant. After all, who wishes upon himself poverty rather than the big winning lottery number?

Who takes pleasure in mourning? That a peaceable nature is good, one can understand, but we do, at least, find it difficult. To hunger and thirst for righteousness, that is certainly a good attitude, but it also points out precisely those situations of scandalous injustices that make one hungry for justice. Mercy is something wonderful when it is shown to us, but we know how difficult it is to be merciful ourselves. Peacemaking is also not something at which we automatically succeed, even if it is perceived to be something very precious.

The final two beatitudes are probably the most difficult. Can anyone be glad about being persecuted for righteousness' sake or even about being cursed for Jesus' sake, persecuted, slandered? How can Jesus call those things "blessed" that cannot help but go against the grain with us? And yet it is peculiar: many people find it to be the case that, right from the beginning of the Sermon on the Mount, of the Beatitudes, an attraction goes forth, a comfort, a fascination, which people of other religions also detect. Even at that time many of his listeners said, "No man ever spoke like this man" (Jn 7:46).

Many promise happiness. Every advertisement promises it. Jesus, however, promises happiness where we would not spontaneously seek it. He promises an indescribable, great happiness. He calls it "blessedness". And he does not say that it is to be had easily and immediately and cheaply. He says, "Your reward is great in heaven." Yes, blessedness is promised us on "the other side", where all sadness will have an end, "up there in heaven".

Karl Marx and his followers made the accusation that this comfort was the "opiate of the people", an anesthetic for enduring this comfortless world, for making the poor content, and for avoiding the need to change anything in this life: It is going badly for you now, but then it will go well with you. So wait patiently for the world hereafter.

But that is precisely what Jesus does not say. He does not put anything off; rather, he changes the world because he changes hearts. And the happiness of which he speaks is not only for "the other side".

However contrary to our inclinations the Beatitudes sound, they also produce at the same time an echo of joy. We suspect that if we were to live as Jesus sums it up in these eight sayings, then the "Blessed are you" would already be a reality now.

The Beatitudes, of course, contain promises for the future. And why should it be bad to have such a perspective of hope for the life after death?

But it is also already true now that God gives comfort to the mourning, that he loves the peacemakers, that anyone who is merciful also experiences God's mercy. A life lived according to the rules of the Sermon on the Mount—that would be the thing that brings happiness. And who seriously believes that the way to happiness is an easy one?

FIFTH SUNDAY IN ORDINARY TIME

The Gospel of Matthew 5:13–16

"You are the salt of the earth; but if salt has lost its taste, how shall its saltiness be restored? It is no longer good for anything except to be thrown out and trodden under foot by men.

"You are the light of the world. A city set on a hill cannot be hidden. Nor do men light a lamp and put it under a bushel, but on a stand, and it gives light to all in the house. Let your light so shine before men, that they may see your good works and give glory to your Father who is in heaven."

❧

Foolish Salt

Nothing is more useless than salt that does not salt. It must be thrown away. Jesus uses this drastic picture as the flipside of a great, powerful saying, "You are the salt of the earth." They must have looked somewhat baffled and sad, the disciples of Jesus, when they heard these words on the Mount of the Beatitudes in Galilee. How are these few fishermen and workmen from Galilee to be, at the same time, salt for all mankind, that is, seasoning? The saying becomes even more puzzling when the second one is added to it: "You are the light of the world." Light, not only for their small

60

environment in poor Galilee, but also for the whole world—is this another example of Oriental exaggeration?

Experience with the words of Jesus teaches us that they are always to be taken very directly and plainly. Jesus is not making a moral appeal to his disciples: Just be the salt of the earth, the light of the world! It would certainly be far too much to expect every person to satisfy such a demand. None of us can be such a great light through our own efforts. Jesus, however, is speaking in the form of a conclusion: You are it, salt and light for the whole world!

We do not understand what Jesus means by that if we look at our own achievements alone. Jesus says of himself, "I am the light of the world." He who believes that Jesus of Nazareth is the Messiah, Christ, the Son of God, will also be able to believe that Jesus truly is "the way, and the truth, and the Life", as he says of himself (Jn 14:6), and that he is this, not for his own people, the Jews, but for all people. That is why Jesus also instructs his disciples to go to all nations and peoples and to bring his light to them, which is what they have done from the beginning and to this day.

Salt is for seasoning; food without salt is tasteless and dull. Life becomes tasty and full of flavor when it contains the salt of Jesus, his word, his loving-kindness, his benevolence, his merciful forgiving, in a word, his love. And Jesus wants this spice of life to reach all men. For this, he needs people who live it and make it visible, who are themselves "salt of the earth".

Quarrelsome, ill-humored, unloving, hard-hearted Christians are as useless as salt that has become, as it literally says in the biblical text, "foolish": nonsensical, stale, and tasteless, in other words. But when they are true disciples of Jesus, then their light in fact shines to all people, whether in their own circle of close friends or whether far beyond this. This is why Jesus says: A city on a hill does not remain hidden. One sees it even from afar. You Christians need not hide. People see you and look at you. People look exactly at what there is to see of you, because being a Christian is not a private matter. It should be visible. For instance, Don Bosco, the great apostle of young people in the nineteenth century, comes to mind. It can be seen from his worldwide impact that Jesus' words about salt and light are no exaggeration.

The Gospel of Matthew 5:17–37

"Do not think that I have come to abolish the law and the prophets; I have come not to abolish them but to fulfil them. For truly, I say to you, till heaven and earth pass away, not an iota, not a dot, will pass from the law until all is accomplished. Whoever then relaxes one of the least of these commandments and teaches men so, shall be called least in the kingdom of heaven; but he who does them and teaches them shall be called great in the kingdom of heaven. For I tell you, unless your righteousness exceeds that of the scribes and Pharisees, you will never enter the kingdom of heaven.

"You have heard that it was said to the men of old, 'You shall not kill; and whoever kills shall be liable to judgment.' But I say to you that every one who is angry with his brother shall be liable to judgment; whoever insults his brother shall be liable to the council, and whoever says, 'You fool!' shall be liable to the hell of fire. So if you are offering your gift at the altar, and there remember that your brother has something against you, leave your gift there before the altar and go; first be reconciled to your brother, and then come and offer your gift. Make friends quickly with your accuser, while you are going with him to court, lest your accuser hand you over to the judge, and the judge to the guard, and you be put in prison; truly, I say to you, you will never get out till you have paid the last penny.

"You have heard that it was said, 'You shall not commit adultery.' But I say to you that every one who looks at a woman lustfully has already committed adultery with her in his heart. If your right eye causes you to sin, pluck it out and throw it away; it is better that you lose one of your members than that your whole body be thrown into hell. And if your right hand causes you to sin, cut it off and throw it away; it is better that you lose one of your members than that your whole body go into hell.

"It was also said, 'Whoever divorces his wife, let him give her a certificate of divorce.' But I say to you that every one who divorces his wife, except on the ground of unchastity, makes her an adulteress; and whoever marries a divorced woman commits adultery.

"Again you have heard that it was said to the men of old, 'You shall not swear falsely, but shall perform to the Lord what you have sworn.' But I say to you, Do not swear at all, either by heaven, for it is the throne of God, or by the earth, for it is his footstool, or by Jerusalem, for it is the city of the great King. And do not swear by your head, for you cannot make one hair white or black. Let what you say be simply 'Yes' or 'No'; anything more than this comes from the Evil One."

❧

A Different System of Values

On Mount Sinai God gave his people and all people through them the ten signposts to life. Whoever does not keep them should not be surprised that disasters come. Do not kill, do not steal, do not lie, do not commit adultery, honor your parents—these are the ABCs of successful living in society. How bad it is when we can no longer trust the word of another person. How terrible it is when there is no place left where we are sure of our lives—how thankful we should be to live in a country where a considerable degree of public safety and order prevails! How destructive it is when there no longer exists a protective fence around the cell of marriage and family, and anybody can invade the relationship, the marriage of another and endanger it—how painfully this is experienced in our country by many couples and even more so by their children! How threatening it is when possessions are no longer secure, when robbery and theft have become so matter of course that the police can only stand idly by and watch—in how many countries of the earth is this a daily reality!

What can be done when the signposts of Mount Sinai, the Ten Commandments, no longer have a determining influence on the life of a people? Many think that only a strong hand, an energetic dictatorship, can restore order in such a situation. History shows, however, that this is seldom the case, that dictators usually make things even worse. The dictatorships of the twentieth century have adequately demonstrated this.

Jesus shows a different way. On the mountain by the Sea of Gennesaret, he establishes new signposts for his disciples and the crowds of people. They clearly go beyond those of Mount Sinai. They do not merely tell what you should not do if you want to win life. They go deeper; they point beyond wrong conduct to the sources of evil conduct. For all the evil, life-destroying deeds prohibited by the Ten Commandments arise from evil thoughts, which at first manifest themselves in evil words before they lead to evil actions.

Jesus prescribes for us a root treatment, and he advises us to begin with ourselves. External compulsory measures will not rehabilitate society (even though they are always necessary for societal life up to a certain extent); rather, there must be a renewal of hearts, of attitudes, of the very foundation of our behavior. Jesus names three areas in which he makes clear his more intensified way.

First, *conflict management*: It is not enough simply to abstain from murder. Much more common is the homicide of the heart, my thoughts of hate, rage, and displeasure at another person, which express themselves in devastating words. Character assassination, wound-causing words need to be combated; they bring about an infinite amount of harm.

Next, *adultery*: It begins with the eyes, in the heart. It begins with our disdaining marriage, the life-relationship with the other person, and deceiving our own spouse long before it comes to outright adultery.

Finally, the *reliability of our words*, our truthfulness: He who resorts to swearing is already acknowledging that he usually does not play straight with the truth. Our hearts should be upright; a Yes should be a Yes; a No should be a No. Only on such honest people can you rely.

Jesus' signposts are aimed at guaranteeing that we do not keep the rules of the Ten Commandments only in an external fashion while making a murderous pit of our hearts. Worldwide I see no better system of values than that presented by Jesus. Wherever it is lived, life again becomes worth living.

SEVENTH SUNDAY IN ORDINARY TIME

The Gospel of Matthew 5:38–48

"You have heard that it was said, 'An eye for an eye and a tooth for a tooth.' But I say to you, Do not resist one who is evil. But if any one strikes you on the right cheek, turn to him the other also; and if any one would sue you and take your coat, let him have your cloak as well; and if any one forces you to go one mile, go with him two miles. Give to him who begs from you, and do not refuse him who would borrow from you.

"You have heard that it was said, 'You shall love your neighbor and hate your enemy.' But I say to you, Love your enemies and pray for those who persecute you, so that you may be sons of your Father who is in heaven; for he makes his sun rise on the evil and on the good, and sends rain on the just and on the unjust. For if you love those who love you, what reward have you? Do not even the tax collectors do the same? And if you salute only your brethren, what more are you doing than others? Do not even the Gentiles do the same? You, therefore, must be perfect, as your heavenly Father is perfect."

Somebody Has to Begin

In the preceding passage of the Sermon on the Mount, Jesus showed the way of a just, upright, good type of behavior,

67

which does not keep only to external rules but is good because it is from the heart and has its source in a right cast of mind.

But what if I indeed behave in such a way while others do not? Precisely this worry concerns us when we hear the Sermon on the Mount: That is, of course, all fine and good—in theory. But in practice, it looks completely different. If I am completely honest in my business life and always tell the truth, will I not then be cheated, taken to the cleaners? And who manages, after all, never to let out an angry or malicious word and to control his eyes to such an extent that he never casts covetous glances?

Today's passage from the Sermon on the Mount seems to intensify this concern even further. Is Jesus demanding here, plainly and simply, something that is humanly impossible: To turn the proverbial "other cheek" when struck on the first one—is that not an excessive demand? And did Jesus himself do what he expects of us? When the court officers struck him on the face, Jesus did not hold out the other cheek; rather, he objected: "If I have spoken wrongly, bear witness to the wrong; but if I have spoken rightly, why do you strike me?" (Jn 18:23).

So did Jesus actually resist the one who did him evil, contrary to his own demand on us? "This order does not mean", so writes the Jesuit biblical scholar P. Klemens Stock, "that one may not oppose the one who does evil, that one may not prevent his actions, that one must stand idly by and is obliged to let every evildoer rage freely and unhindered".[1]

The policeman who stands in the way of a bank robber may not turn the other cheek. He must arrest him, with

[1] P. Klemens, *Jesus—Kinder der Seligkeit* (Innsbruck and Vienna, 1991), p. 50.

force of arms, if necessary. I have a right to defend myself with legal means against an injustice that befalls me. But Jesus' question aims at our hearts: Do you claim your right out of feelings of vengeance, out of injured self-love, out of an attitude of always having to be right at all costs?

The Apostle Paul tells us what it is all about: "See that none of you repays evil for evil, but always seek to do good to one another and to all" (1 Thess 5:15). That is also the point of the most difficult of all the commandments of Jesus: "Love your enemies and pray for those who persecute you." Jesus does not demand of us that we foster feelings of affection or sympathy for our enemies. That would of course be against human nature. What Jesus expects, though, is that we do not wish on our enemy the evil that he inflicts on us. We should stop the cycle of evil, break through the spiral of violence: "Do not be overcome by evil, but overcome evil with good" (Rom 12:21).

To love wherever we encounter love is nothing special. We find that easy. But to have goodwill toward the one who does us evil, this makes us like God, who is good to all whether they thank him or not. Moreover, history and our own experience show one thing: Revenge has never brought about peace. Somebody has to make the beginning of venturing the step toward the other person. And Jesus thinks that I should be that somebody.

Eighth Sunday in Ordinary Time

The Gospel of Matthew 6:24–34

"No one can serve two masters; for either he will hate the one and love the other, or he will be devoted to the one and despise the other. You cannot serve God and mammon.

"Therefore I tell you, do not be anxious about your life, what you shall eat or what you shall drink, nor about your body, what you shall put on. Is not life more than food, and the body more than clothing? Look at the birds of the air: they neither sow nor reap nor gather into barns, and yet your heavenly Father feeds them. Are you not of more value than they? And which of you by being anxious can add one cubit to his span of life? And why are you anxious about clothing? Consider the lilies of the field, how they grow; they neither toil nor spin; yet I tell you, even Solomon in all his glory was not clothed like one of these. But if God so clothes the grass of the field, which today is alive and tomorrow is thrown into the oven, will he not much more clothe you, O you of little faith? Therefore do not be anxious, saying, 'What shall we eat?' or 'What shall we drink?' or 'What shall we wear?' For the Gentiles seek all these things; and your heavenly Father knows that you need them all. But seek first his kingdom and his righteousness, and all these things shall be yours as well.

"Therefore do not be anxious about tomorrow, for tomorrow will be anxious for itself. Let the day's own trouble be sufficient for the day."

No One Cares Like That

Does not Jesus do exactly the thing of which Karl Marx accuses religion: It is an opiate of the people—that is, an anesthetic and an intoxicant that is supposed to let you forget the poverty in this life and hope for better in the next world. Are not such words more likely to hinder people from taking their fate into their own hands and building a better future? Would there have been such a successful rebuilding after the war if all these words of Jesus had been followed? "Do not be anxious about tomorrow"—is that not more cynical than helpful, especially when we consider that Jesus' many listeners at that time in Galilee on the Mount of the Beatitudes were mostly poor, very poor people.

Now, we must certainly assume that Jesus thought about the morrow in his hidden years as a carpenter in Nazareth. How in any workshop he also had to make provision for the future, store materials, obtain and replace tools, probably also make cost estimates, and then make sure that he kept to them. All of this calls for planning, calculation, foresight, and care. He could not do it like the "birds of the air" or the "lilies of the field", which do not need all of that. Did he therefore live differently from what he preached?

I think Jesus is concerned about something else. He is not against planning and looking ahead. He certainly does not mean to say we should abstain from sowing and reaping and simply take each day as it comes. He does not set us that example. His six-times repeated call: "Do not be anxious!" means anxious concern, not industrious provision. He wants us to pursue our work free of fear and full of confidence. That is why he gives us very concrete directions. God takes care of nature; how much more will he look after us, his children.

Thanks to the modern methods of science and the media, we can understand much more about the mystery of creation today. How elaborately, how wonderfully everything in the plant and animal world is arranged! Who on earth can come close to inventing or even manufacturing such things? We can only marvel at it all. So should God not look at us in the same way and even more so?

But where does our lack of trust in God come from? Why are our cares often so anxious, our faith so small? Because we have not chosen clearly enough; we might want to serve God, but we want to serve mammon as well. We want to trust God, but not completely. Our anxious care comes from this half-heartedness. How will things be tomorrow? How will it all work out? Will we have something to eat? How many people in Africa live with this question every day? And how many in our country have to ask themselves whether they will manage to pay their bills next month? How does trust in God help toward that end? I am thinking, above all, in two directions: He who trusts in God will not put an excessive amount of trust in money and will rather go the path of modesty and moderation. Mammon is an insatiable master. Whoever serves it never gets enough and runs into many worries. Whoever trusts in God will be content with the bare necessities and will thus find peace.

Whoever strives to serve God will, moreover, experience time and again how closely and attentively God stands by us, even in the smallest things, and lets us know that he is our Father, who really cares for us, like no other.

NINTH SUNDAY IN ORDINARY TIME

The Gospel of Matthew 7:21–27

*"Not every one who says to me, 'Lord, Lord,' shall enter
the kingdom of heaven, but he who does the will of my
Father who is in heaven. On that day many will say to
me, 'Lord, Lord, did we not prophesy in your name, and
cast out demons in your name, and do many mighty works
in your name?' And then will I declare to them, 'I never
knew you; depart from me, you evildoers.'*

*"Every one then who hears these words of mine and does
them will be like a wise man who built his house upon the
rock; and the rain fell, and the floods came, and the winds
blew and beat upon that house, but it did not fall, because
it had been founded on the rock. And every one who hears
these words of mine and does not do them will be like a foolish man who built his house upon the sand; and the rain
fell, and the floods came, and the winds blew and beat against
that house, and it fell; and great was the fall of it."*

*And when Jesus finished these sayings, the crowds were
astonished at his teaching, for he taught them as one who
had authority, and not as their scribes.*

&

Build the House of Your Life!

Life is like the building of a house. If anyone builds on
solid ground, then his life-house will hold in storms and

73

inclement weather. If anyone has built on sand, then that person's house may indeed look beautiful, may be luxuriously furnished, but then it will not offer shelter and security when they are especially needed: in difficult times, when crises shake his life, storms beat against it, and floods descend upon him.

Jesus' little parable about the two homebuilders, the wise one and the foolish one, reminds us that what matters in life is first and fundamentally the foundation. The most beautiful structure is of no use in an emergency if the foundation cannot carry it.

Whether everything is in order or not, whether it is solid rock or loose sand, cannot be seen from the façade because the foundation is not visible. It proves itself in an emergency, and, for emergencies, it is necessary to take precautions.

On what am I building the house of my life then? Jesus says very simply and clearly: You can build your life on your will or on God's will. Whoever trusts in his own will has built on sand, because our will is weak, wavering, it gives in easily and lets itself be upset by small storms. Whoever bases his life on God's will stands firm; he will not lose confidence even in difficult crises, will not collapse; he can hold on tightly to God.

But how do I know what God's will is? Jesus also gives a simple answer here: Keep my word! Follow the Gospel; it tells you what God wants; it shows you the solid foundation for your life-house. On this foundation you can confidently build your life.

You must, however, do your own building. God shows you a good foundation; he puts it at your disposal: Jesus' word is this foundation. On this you are building when you actually do his will, when you not only hear the words of Jesus but act in accordance with them as well. It is not words, but deeds, that count. It is not the one who says "Lord! Lord!" to Jesus who is a disciple of Jesus; rather, it is the one who lives according to his word, the one who makes it visible in his life.

Nor do many pious acts help if we only use them to indulge in self-adulation and to boast about our religious achievements: "I do not know you", Jesus says brusquely to this. Jesus often indicates which people he knows and particularly loves: the simple, upright, selfless people, no matter whether small or great, rich or poor. What matters to him is not the beautiful façade of the house; what matters is the heart, the hands that do what is necessary, that do not look at themselves first but, instead, look at the well-being of others. Others will also find shelter and security in the life-house of the person who builds in this way.

The Gospel of Matthew 9:9–13

As Jesus passed on from there, he saw a man called Matthew sitting at the tax office; and he said to him, "Follow me." And he rose and followed him.

And as he sat at table in the house, behold, many tax collectors and sinners came and sat down with Jesus and his disciples. And when the Pharisees saw this, they said to his disciples, "Why does your teacher eat with tax collectors and sinners?" But when he heard it, he said, "Those who are well have no need of a physician, but those who are sick. Go and learn what this means, 'I desire mercy, and not sacrifice.' For I came not to call the righteous, but sinners."

ﻉﺍ

I Desire Mercy!

Images from the everyday life of the stock exchange can be seen in the media over and over again: "speculators", brokers, hectically telephoning, a loud babble of voices, and everything revolves around stock prices, profits, and losses. Things might not have been quite as hectic at the tax office where a Jew named Levi, or Matthew, worked. It was located not far from Capernaum on the great trade route that led from the East to the Mediterranean.

Jesus passes by this place. His eye falls on Matthew. Why on him; why not on someone else, everyone else? We do not know. This is Jesus' sovereign freedom. But Matthew's life is different from that moment. Anyone who has felt the call of God in his life can understand this. God does not just somehow look from "up there" generally on us "down here", on the tangled mass in our earthly world. There are moments in life when God comes by, almost in person I would like to say, looks at me, at me very personally, in the middle of my business dealings, in the turmoil of my everyday life, and speaks directly to me: Follow me!

For Matthew this is the decisive point in his life. To be concise, this means that he stands up from his tax post and follows Jesus. The one who writes this is that man himself, the apostle and later evangelist Matthew. He knows like no one else what a change the encounter with Jesus brings into his life.

The religious people do not immediately see the change in his life. So they get upset (which is not entirely incomprehensible!) about the fact that Jesus invites this tax collector into his home and holds a banquet for him and his friends. Joining together around the table was a strong sign of acceptance and friendship at that time. How can your Master sit at the same table with such bad people? The Pharisees are honestly trying hard to lead decent and devout lives, and that is why they often bring rich sacrifices and give up many an economic advantage. Indeed, it is hard, even today, to keep the commandments of God in everyday life, with taxes, in politics. That is why the agitation of the Pharisees is all too easy to understand.

Jesus' answer is simple and clear, and yet it demands an enormous change of thinking: Those who are sick need a physician. Anyone who leads a life like this Matthew is spiritually sick, even though that person earns a lot of money. And Jesus wants him to get to know a life different from just having as much money as possible in his purse. It is good to lead a respectable life; in fact, it is very good. But it must not lead to despising others.

Jesus desires mercy, not arrogance. How could any of us, no matter how respectably we live, get along without the mercy of God and that of other people as well?

The Gospel of Matthew 9:36–10:8

When he saw the crowds, he had compassion for them, because they were harassed and helpless, like sheep without a shepherd. Then he said to his disciples, "The harvest is plentiful, but the laborers are few; pray therefore the Lord of the harvest to send out laborers into his harvest."

And he called to him his twelve disciples and gave them authority over unclean spirits, to cast them out, and to heal every disease and every infirmity. The names of the twelve apostles are these: first, Simon, who is called Peter, and Andrew his brother; James the son of Zebedee, and John his brother; Philip and Bartholomew; Thomas and Matthew the tax collector; James the son of Alphaeus, and Thaddaeus; Simon the Cananaean, and Judas Iscariot, who betrayed him.

These Twelve Jesus sent out, charging them, "Go nowhere among the Gentiles, and enter no town of the Samaritans, but go rather to the lost sheep of the house of Israel. And preach as you go, saying, 'The kingdom of heaven is at hand.' Heal the sick, raise the dead, cleanse lepers, cast out demons. You received without pay, give without pay."

ès

The Harvest Is Great

When Jesus looks at us, he sees us differently from the way we see ourselves and each other.

He sees our situation as more serious and at the same time as more promising than we perceive it to be.

This means that Jesus is moved by a compassion coming from his innermost heart when he sees the many people around him. We, too, see much need around us. Jesus looks deeper. He knows about the hidden needs that others do not notice. He sees our exhaustion, the weakness of our lives, which is often concealed behind the façade of busyness and entertainment. We are inclined to believe that everything is going reasonably well. Jesus sees the lack of direction in our lives, which hurry along without our really knowing where they are leading or why: "like sheep without shepherds".

Does Jesus see us too pessimistically? His compassion for us is just the flip side of a great hope: "The harvest is great." Jesus sees everything we have in us: how many talents there would be but for their lying undeveloped; how much could grow, could become reality if the unfolding of it all were not hindered; how many wounds could be healed if they were treated; how much life, fulfilled life, God wants to give if only there were a breakthrough: "The harvest is great!"

It is like an outcry of the heart when Jesus adds: "But there are too few laborers!"

It hurts to see how rich the harvest of fulfilled life would be if only God had enough co-workers to help gather it in. That is why we should ask God, the "Lord of the harvest", for such workers.

Who are they, these harvest workers? What should we pray for? Jesus straightaway gives the answer himself by calling the Twelve, so that they could be such harvest workers of God. These twelve men, whom we call the apostles because they are the ones who were sent out by Jesus (this is what the word apostle means), are to be messengers of hope; they are to help people get free of the clutches of evil, bring physical and spiritual healing, and they are to begin first of all in their own land, in their own nation of Israel.

Jesus called the first Twelve to himself at that time. Does he still do this today as well? And are people today ready, like the first Twelve, to let themselves be taken into service as God's harvest workers? Without a doubt, God is calling people today. And thank God that, even today, there are many who are ready for service, often without many words, as a matter of course and selflessly. Such people make our world warmer and kinder.

But Jesus' complaint is valid even today: There are too few helping hands and hearts of this type, considering the great spiritual need of our time. It is a painful mystery to me why in our country—unlike other countries—we do not have more vocations to the priesthood, especially when this service still stands in the succession of the apostles, whom Jesus called to be the first. Perhaps we must learn to see anew how great the harvest is in order to comprehend again how beautiful it is to dedicate one's life completely to this task.

TWELFTH SUNDAY IN ORDINARY TIME

The Gospel of Matthew 10:26–33

"So have no fear of them; for nothing is covered that will not be revealed, or hidden that will not be known. What I tell you in the dark, utter in the light; and what you hear whispered, proclaim upon the housetops. And do not fear those who kill the body but cannot kill the soul; rather fear him who can destroy both soul and body in hell. Are not two sparrows sold for a penny? And not one of them will fall to the ground without your Father's will. But even the hairs of your head are all numbered. Fear not, therefore; you are of more value than many sparrows. So every one who acknowledges me before men, I also will acknowledge before my Father who is in heaven; but whoever denies me before men, I also will deny before my Father who is in heaven."

❧

Even the Sparrows

Three times Jesus calls out to his listeners today: "Have no fear!" What are we not to fear? To have no fear at all would probably not be the right thing. Because there is a lot that quite naturally frightens us as human beings. We are afraid of anything that threatens us and anything against which we feel powerless. Many people have to be anxious about their jobs today with more and more jobs being "stream-lined away". Worrying about health can be a heavy bur-den, as are problems in relationships, marriage crises, and the accompanying loss of security that threatens. At its deep-est level, it is probably the fear of losing what is dear to us. And because everything in this world is transitory, every-thing is always and everywhere endangered as well, and from this comes so much of the fear in our lives.

It is just this fear that we should overcome, even if it seems almost impossible. Jesus gives three steps for doing this. The fear of rubbing people the wrong way is the first thing to overcome. It often cripples us from expressing our convictions. This prevents many Christians from publicly answering for their faith. What Jesus said should come out and not remain in the sacristy, because his good news should reach all people. That is why Christians should not fear professing their faith in Christ before others, so that one day he will not have to say to them: "I do not know you!"

With this, we are now at the second "Have no fear." Only one loss is really to be feared: losing God. For who-ever loses him loses everything. Whoever has him cannot be harmed by any other loss.

I will never forget meeting a campmate of Alexander Solzhenitsyn. In the Siberian Gulag, according to his expe-rience, the ones who were most likely to survive were those who did not strive to maintain their physical survival at all costs, those who feared the death of the soul more than that of the body. Viktor Frankl experienced something sim-ilar in Auschwitz.

Death, which is certain for us all, is not the greatest evil. It is worse to lose one's soul, to become heartless. Whoever fearlessly gives his life to fight for good, for others, and for God does not need to fear death.

How can such inner freedom be won? Jesus' third "Have no fear" shows the way: Trust in God! Your Father in heaven knows what you need. He cares for all of you, down to your very hairs. He loves even the sparrows and, how much more, you! Teresa of Avila speaks to this attitude in a famous poem:

> Let nothing trouble you,
> Let nothing frighten you,
> Everything passes.
> God never changes.
> Patience
> Obtains all.
> Whoever has God
> Wants for nothing.
> God alone is enough.

The Gospel of Matthew 10:37–42

"He who loves father or mother more than me is not worthy of me; and he who loves son or daughter more than me is not worthy of me; and he who does not take his cross and follow me is not worthy of me. He who finds his life will lose it, and he who loses his life for my sake will find it.

"He who receives you receives me, and he who receives me receives him who sent me. He who receives a prophet because he is a prophet shall receive a prophet's reward, and he who receives a righteous man because he is a righteous man shall receive a righteous man's reward. And whoever gives to one of these little ones even a cup of cold water because he is a disciple, truly, I say to you, he shall not lose his reward."

૨৯

Love of Parents—Love of God

Honor your father and mother, so reads the fourth of the Ten Commandments.

That fathers and mothers love their children especially, more than they love all other people, is natural, because there are no closer blood ties than those between parents and children. For this reason, there is also the special, holy obligation to honor and respect our own parents, who gave us life. It is also natural for us to be attached to our parents and for their loss to be profoundly painful.

Nevertheless, Jesus says that it is a condition for becoming his disciple to love him more than we do even our own parents and our own children. Is not such a demand inhuman; is it not excessive, plain and simple? Can a man demand such total attachment?

Is that not the manner of gurus in sects, who expect total submission from their followers?

Jesus' words in today's Gospel would be excessive in every respect, presumptuous, deserving of being categorically rejected, if Jesus had been only a man. No man can demand that others set him above all natural human ties.

The words are instantly meaningful if Jesus really is the Son of God. Only God stands above man. He is the only one we can and should love more than even those we hold dearest. We see what this can mean whenever young people feel the call to imitate Christ completely, as priests, as nuns. Then it happens time and again that the parents put up fierce resistance, that they are afraid of losing their child and are not prepared to bring this sacrifice and offer it to God. For the one who feels the call of Jesus, it then comes to a painful decision between the imitation of Christ and the attachment to parents. Today there would certainly be more priestly vocations and more new members in religious orders if more parents were ready joyfully and thankfully to accept such a call in the lives of their children and to support that call.

By the way, experience shows that God rewards such a sacrifice. Many parents of priests and of members of religious orders can attest to the fact that they have not lost their child but have, on the contrary, been richly rewarded. Their sacrifice has become a blessing to them.

The other saying of Jesus comes true here: He who anxiously and egotistically clings to his life and everything dear to him will lose it. He who confidently places everything in God's hand will win his life, even when God demands sacrifice. This even applies to the cross that I have to carry in my life if I say Yes to it.

It is inevitable that we experience sorrow in life, that we have the yoke of a cross to carry. The question is always new: How will I face it?

Do I balk at it? Nothing is more natural than to fight against sorrow. But what if all resistance is useless? How impressive it is when people courageously accept their cross from God's hand! Then things can even change—into profound joy.

The Gospel of Matthew 11:25–30

At that time Jesus declared, "I thank thee, Father, Lord of heaven and earth, that you have hidden these things from the wise and understanding and revealed them to infants; yes, Father, for such was your gracious will. All things have been delivered to me by my Father; and no one knows the Son except the Father, and no one knows the Father except the Son and any one to whom the Son chooses to reveal him. Come to me, all who labor and are heavy laden, and I will give you rest. Take my yoke upon you, and learn from me; for I am gentle and lowly in heart, and you will find rest for your souls. For my yoke is easy, and my burden is light."

≥a

Come to Me

Today's Gospel is one of the most beautiful, most precious passages of the entire Bible. Jesus allows us a deep look into his innermost heart. He opens his heart and shows what moves him.

Immediately preceding this passage, Jesus laments in serious words about the unbelief of his countrymen who saw so many signs and wonders from him and nevertheless gave him no credence. As much as this ingratitude pains him, he nevertheless also finds reason for joy, and our Gospel today speaks of this.

Something the Gospels seldom report: Jesus begins to pray loudly in front of everyone. They are words full of joy and gratitude. They let us sense where and who the source is from which he draws his power. The fundamental basis of his life is the one he simply calls "Father", "Lord of heaven and earth".

"I thank you, Father!" These words have a unique ring to them. It is the joy found in God that rings out here. Compared to it, there is no greater joy. And no one knows it more than Jesus. Because, as Christians confess on the basis of today's Gospel, no man has ever been so completely one with God as Jesus. Only he can say of himself that he really knows God the Father. And we cannot comprehend on our own who Jesus really is, because only the Father knows him through and through. That is why Christians are convinced that Jesus is the Son of God, true God and true man.

To the "wise and understanding", as Jesus calls them, all this seems unbelievable. But as for the simple, the upright, the small and despised, their hearts rise when they meet Jesus.

The secret of Jesus' power of attraction became clearer to me through Padre Pio, whom the Pope canonized on June 16, 2002, in Rome. I had the chance to meet him myself in 1961. I will never forget how he celebrated Holy Mass. It was no longer merely an external ritual; that Padre Pio truly experienced what took place there in the Mass was tangible.

Why do seven million people a year make a pilgrimage to his tomb even today? I believe his absolute closeness to God makes him so incredibly attractive to people. They experience him as a helper to whom they can go to with all their problems.

That is the reason Jesus calls out to people: Come to me, all who labor and are heavy laden. He promises what he alone can do. With him, my heart finds rest, more than can be found in all the wellness and fitness centers with their contributions to physical well-being. But he can relieve me of the burdens that weigh upon my soul. Of course, only under one condition: I must be prepared to learn from him and to take his yoke upon myself. Just as there is no physical fitness training without one's own participation, so Jesus can give us his "refreshment" only if we take on his "program". Compared with the troubles we are prepared to take upon ourselves for health and success, his "yoke" is actually not heavy. It is, quite simply: Love God and your neighbor.

The Gospel of Matthew 13:1–9

That same day Jesus went out of the house and sat beside the sea. And great crowds gathered about him, so that he got into a boat and sat there; and the whole crowd stood on the beach. And he told them many things in parables, saying: "A sower went out to sow. And as he sowed, some seeds fell along the path, and the birds came and devoured them. Other seeds fell on rocky ground, where they had not much soil, and immediately they sprang up, since they had no depth of soil, but when the sun rose they were scorched; and since they had no root they withered away. Other seeds fell upon thorns, and the thorns grew up and choked them. Other seeds fell on good soil and brought forth grain, some a hundredfold, some sixty, some thirty. He who has ears, let him hear."

(Complete text: Mt 13:1–23)

༃

A Sower Went out to the Field

He who has ears, let him hear! Jesus expressed much of what he wanted to say to people in parables. Stories make a better impression on the mind than abstract teachings. Who does not remember the parable of the prodigal son, who returns to his merciful father, or the parable of the Good Samaritan?

People clearly enjoyed listening to Jesus whenever he spoke to them and told them parables, as in today's Gospel, and they enjoyed listening to him at length. Jesus gripped their attention not only because he was able to tell such fascinating stories. In his parables, he always addressed a decision, a change in the lives of his listeners. The parables should strike the heart and awaken a readiness to change one's thinking and one's ways. They do not allow you to be neutral. They make clear what I myself should and can change, and they give us confidence that there will be success. For the parables of Jesus always talk about the "kingdom of heaven", which means what God does, how he intervenes and helps, if we are alert to it.

A sower goes out to a field to sow. That is how the story begins. All the listeners know what it is talking about, how sowing was done then and how barren and poor most of the soil in the Holy Land was. But the sower of whom Jesus is talking has two unusual qualities. He sows liberally to the point of being wasteful, and, contrary to all agricultural common sense, he sows on all types of soil, on the road, on rocky ground, in the thorny undergrowth. It is no surprise that the seed quickly goes to waste in those places. It is, however, astonishing that the good soil does not, as was common at the time, produce at most ten times the seed sown but instead produces the unimaginable return of thirty, sixty, even one hundredfold. Despite all the failure on the bad soil, overall a "super harvest" is nevertheless achieved, over and above anything naturally possible.

We are the soil. The sower is Christ. God himself gives the chance of yield.

Jesus is directly asking me the decisive question: How does the field of your life look? Are you as inaccessible to

God's word as a hard-trod path on which the seeds remain lying? Does the soil of your life have too little depth, so that it suffices for a short moment of enthusiasm, but, when the heat of the day comes with its difficulties and obstacles, then there is a lack of endurance, of staying power? Or are you like the thorny, overgrown soil, where the weeds overpower the good seed because all the other things—the worries of everyday life, the distractions, your own interests— have driven God's word and working out of your life?

The story of the unusual sower is a mirror Jesus holds up to us. But the sober look in the mirror is not supposed to be discouraging. For God can change the soil of my life. He can plough it up; he can break up my lumps and turn my life, overgrown with weeds, into fertile farmland. I have only to let him work, open myself to his word, be prepared for him to plough up my life. That can be painful. But only in this way will my life become productive. And that is why Jesus came: A sower went out to sow . . .

SIXTEENTH SUNDAY IN ORDINARY TIME

The Gospel of Matthew 13:24–30

Another parable he put before them, saying, "The kingdom of heaven may be compared to a man who sowed good seed in his field; but while men were sleeping, his enemy came and sowed weeds among the wheat, and went away. So when the plants came up and bore grain, then the weeds appeared also. And the servants of the householder came and said to him, 'Sir, did you not sow good seed in your field? How then has it weeds?' He said to them, 'An enemy has done this.' The servants said to him, 'Then do you want us to go and gather them?' But he said, 'No; lest in gathering the weeds you root up the wheat along with them. Let both grow together until the harvest; and at harvest time I will tell the reapers, Gather the weeds first and bind them in bundles to be burned, but gather the wheat into my barn.' "

(Complete text: Mt 13:24–43)

৯৯

Weeds Do Perish

Who is not familiar with it, that annoying mixture of good seed and undesired weeds?

In every garden, one must take great pains to keep the weeds from overgrowing everything else. A well-tended

94

garden therefore has to be weeded regularly so that the weeds do not gain the upper hand. The longer one waits, the more difficult it becomes to keep them under control. That is why the essential thing in garden care is: Always stick to it!

It is no different in our lives. If I do not clear away the ever-returning weeds in my soul every day, then they will quickly overgrow the good aspects of my being. Bad habits must be continually combated; otherwise, they develop roots so strong that they become indestructible. Education from an early age is the alpha and omega of a successful life. He who has learned from childhood on not simply to give in to his bad inclinations but to fight them bravely and ever anew, that person will become quite pleasant to his fellow-man, like the well-tended garden of a neighbor.

Jesus seems fully to contradict all this in today's parable: Let the weeds grow with the wheat! That almost sounds like a program for "anti-authoritarian education", which was fashionable in the 'seventies. At that time many people, especially the "progressives", thought: If you just let the children have their own way in everything, then they will surely turn out well on their own accord. Many "modern" parents and their children soon had to find out painfully that this is not at all how it works.

What does Jesus mean to say with this parable? And what does he not mean to say with it? Certainly he does not want us to lose the courage to battle the evil in us. Certainly he does not want us to despair over the fact that there will always be weeds as long as we live in this world.

Jesus is talking about the kingdom of heaven. With this, he means the community he came to establish and build up. In this community of Jesus, in the Church, in Christianity, there will also always be the weeds of the unchristian next to the good wheat sown by Christ. This is not pleasant, and almost every day negative reports in the media remind us that there are many weeds among Christians. Moreover, Jesus says clearly where they come from: An enemy has done this to me—the devil does not sleep, and he especially has his eye on the work of Jesus.

Even if it is painful and annoying to see weeds now growing in the good wheat of Christianity, have patience and be confident: Weeds do perish! God himself will take care of that at harvest time.

But for the time being it is necessary to wait. Many people think they can already reap everything neatly and tidily now and can tell exactly what is good wheat and what are weeds. "Let both grow together until the harvest", Jesus says. "And at harvest time I will tell the reapers: Gather the weeds first and bind them in bundles to be burned, but gather the wheat into my barn."

It will never be possible before then to eradicate all evil. In our hearts, among us men and women, good and bad will always be found at the same time—mixed, just like the weeds that grow in the wheat field. But one day God himself will intervene. Good will then triumph. Until then, we are in a probationary period.

Seventeenth Sunday in Ordinary Time

The Gospel of Matthew 13:44–52

"The kingdom of heaven is like treasure hidden in a field, which a man found and covered up; then in his joy he goes and sells all that he has and buys that field.

"Again, the kingdom of heaven is like a merchant in search of fine pearls, who, on finding one pearl of great value, went and sold all that he had and bought it.

"Again, the kingdom of heaven is like a net which was thrown into the sea and gathered fish of every kind; when it was full, men drew it ashore and sat down and sorted the good into vessels but threw away the bad. So it will be at the close of the age. The angels will come out and separate the evil from the righteous, and throw them into the furnace of fire, where there will be weeping and gnashing of teeth.

"Have you understood all this?" They said to him, "Yes." And he said to them, "Therefore every scribe who has been trained for the kingdom of heaven is like a householder who brings out of his treasure what is new and what is old."

❧

The Most Valuable Find

The parables of Jesus have made such a deep impression on the generations that they have often become proverbial. This is true for the little parable about the treasure in the field as

97

well. In two short sentences, everything is said. In a field he does not own, a man discovers a treasure, which is even less his property. He probably works in the field as a poor day laborer and comes upon the buried treasure while working. The owner of the field knows nothing about the treasure. The man does not even think of informing the owner about the valuable find. He himself wants to be the happy one, so he sells what he has and buys the field from the unsuspecting landowner. "In his joy", Jesus says, and with that he gives the story its decisive keyword.

Is Jesus not praising immoral conduct here? Even if the lucky finder had lawfully acquired the field, the seller definitely must have felt deceived. Now it is certainly not Jesus' intention to tell a "moral tale". Instead, he is talking about the "kingdom of heaven". He who finds this has "hit the jackpot", has had a stroke of great luck. But in contrast to the lottery, the finder of the treasure must take a necessary step: buy the field. And for this day laborer, that means selling everything, really everything, so that he can raise the purchase price for the field.

This necessary step becomes even clearer in the second little parable. The pearl merchant sees the chance of acquiring *the* pearl of great value, the one every pearl merchant dreams of, like the "blue Mauritius" for stamp collectors, so to speak. Without hesitation, he sells what he has in order to buy it. It is worth everything else to him; to him it is *the* deal of his life. With it, he has made his fortune.

He who finds "the kingdom of heaven" experiences a feeling of happiness like the finder of the treasure, an enthusiasm like that of the pearl merchant. The "kingdom of heaven" is no other than Jesus himself. He is the treasure in the field, the pearl of great value. To discover him is *the* luck of my life, but only if I, too, actually stake *everything* in order to gain him. Winning Jesus is not like winning a lucky lottery number: I win Jesus at the price of exchanging everything else for him. The exchange is worth it; the gain is incomparable. But it costs the full commitment.

To want to have both will not work: my little bit of pleasure and glory, which I can win for myself from life; and him, who is more precious than everything. Both parables culminate in a risky, daring action; they challenge you to take a courageous leap of faith. Half-hearted people do not manage it. Anyone who stakes a little on God and a little on his own little money purse will never experience the happiness to which Jesus invites us today.

Joy is the keyword of this Gospel. The treasure finder and the pearl merchant joyfully sell everything they have. Christians should be recognizable by this joy. For they have truly made the most valuable find. How sad it is when someone finds it and then, nevertheless, does not take hold of it.

The Gospel of Matthew 14:13–21

Now when Jesus heard this, he withdrew from there in a boat to a lonely place apart. But when the crowds heard it, they followed him on foot from the towns. As he went ashore he saw a great throng; and he had compassion on them, and healed their sick. When it was evening, the disciples came to him and said, "This is a lonely place, and the day is now over; send the crowds away to go into the villages and buy food for themselves." Jesus said, "They need not go away; you give them something to eat." They said to him, "We have only five loaves here and two fish." And he said, "Bring them here to me." Then he ordered the crowds to sit down on the grass; and taking the five loaves and the two fish he looked up to heaven, and blessed, and broke and gave the loaves to the disciples, and the disciples gave them to the crowds. And they all ate and were satisfied. And they took up twelve baskets full of the broken pieces left over. And those who ate were about five thousand men, besides women and children.

೪

Much More Than I Have

Jesus wants to be alone. The Gospel begins with this today. Why he is drawn into this solitude, the Evangelist has already related. John the Baptist, his relative and his "forerunner", has been brutally beheaded. The motive for this was sordid: one of Herod's drinking bouts, during which the daughter from his wife's first marriage danced. His wife was Herodias, whom the king had "stolen" from his brother Philip. Herodias could not forgive John for saying openly and clearly that this was wrong and was forbidden. The dance pleased Herod, and in his uninhibited wine-altered mood, he offered the daughter a free wish. Herodias seized the chance and advised her daughter: Demand the head of John! And since Herod was cowardly, he did not withstand even this injustice.

John died because he had the courage of the old prophets to call a spade a spade, even when it was an injustice concerning the ruler, regardless of whether it was out of place or not. Jesus knows that the same road is in store for him. But his hour has not yet come, and so he draws back into solitude.

And just as the simple people loved and honored John because of his courage and his credibility, so, too, do they honor Jesus. They run after him, seek him, want to see, hear, touch him, hope for comfort and maybe even healing from him.

While Jesus can be hard on the arrogance and hardheartedness of the self-righteous, at the same time he is quite moved by the way the poor and the simple folk are fondly attached to him and seek his help. He has compassion on them and heals many of the sick. The Evangelist Mark adds that Jesus teaches the people for many hours, until it is evening. He does not want to free the people from their illnesses alone; he also wants, above all, to show them the right way and to impart full trust in his God and Father to them.

His own disciples' trust in God is strongly put to the test in the process. They have practical minds: It is late; the people have to eat (and so do they!). "So send them home at last, away from here, where there is nothing to eat!" This contrast always moves me: Jesus attracts the people; the disciples want to send them away. But Jesus wants his disciples to take after his heart completely. Do not send the people away! Nor, indeed, should you drive them away! "*You* give them something to eat!" Jesus says. I feel this to be a lasting challenge of Jesus to his disciples. They rightly feel that too much is being asked of them: so many people—and so little in our hands! But then they find that the more they distribute the bread blessed by Jesus, the more it multiplies in their hands, until in the end twelve baskets full of broken pieces are left over.

I firmly believe that this miracle of the multiplication of the loaves actually took place. It has been repeated in the lives of so many saints (for example, in the life of Saint Dominic, in the life of the Curé of Ars). But it is also repeated as a daily occurrence: He who gives Jesus his own few gifts and talents finds that God multiplies them. And then I can give much more than I myself have. This is the continual experience we have when we love our neighbor.

Nineteenth Sunday in Ordinary Time

The Gospel of Matthew 14:22–33

Then he made the disciples get into the boat and go before him to the other side, while he dismissed the crowds. And after he had dismissed the crowds, he went up into the hills by himself to pray. When evening came, he was there alone, but the boat by this time was many furlongs distant from the land, beaten by the waves; for the wind was against them. And in the fourth watch of the night he came to them, walking on the sea. But when the disciples saw him walking on the sea, they were terrified, saying, "It is a ghost!" And they cried out for fear. But immediately he spoke to them, saying, "Take heart, it is I; have no fear."

And Peter answered him, "Lord, if it is you, bid me come to you on the water." He said, "Come." So Peter got out of the boat and walked on the water and came to Jesus; but when he saw the wind, he was afraid, and beginning to sink he cried out, "Lord, save me." Jesus immediately reached out his hand and caught him, saying to him, "O you of little faith, why did you doubt?" And when they got into the boat, the wind ceased. And those in the boat worshiped him, saying, "Truly you are the Son of God."

❧

Thank You, Peter!

On the hill above Tabga, the place of the miraculous multiplication of the loaves, there is a cave. Local tradition says that Jesus withdrew into this cave to pray in solitude. From this small grotto, a magnificent view over the entire Sea of Gennesaret is offered. With this, we can well understand the setting of today's Gospel. While the disciples are already in their boat on the sea, probably traveling homeward in the direction of Capernaum, Jesus takes leave of the many people who have followed him on foot to this lonely place on the seacoast and who, for their part, are now returning home, richly rewarded with what they have heard and received from Jesus.

But where is Jesus at home? Where does he rest after work completed? It says he remained there alone on the seacoast and withdrew to the mountain overlooking the sea, "by himself to pray". If we want to get to know Jesus, then we will best find him where his heart is, where he is at home: in intimate contact with God, whom he calls "Father". He lives from this center; he draws his power from this source.

Alone, on the mountain with God, he nevertheless does not lose sight of his own. He sees how they row with difficulty, for in the meantime one of the frequent severe winds arises that make the sea so dangerous even today. I think this holds true to this day: Jesus, who is now completely with the Father, continues to see that we have difficult rowing to do and that we make progress in the ship of our lives only with difficulty as the storms of life press upon us.

And then Jesus comes to them, but not straightaway, not in order to remove every trouble immediately. Until the fourth, final night watch—that is, right up to the end of the night, shortly before the break of dawn—he lets them struggle with the turbulent sea. Could he not have helped earlier? Why does he wait so long, why does he leave us—seemingly—alone in our need? We see only our own distress in such stormy hours, whereas he watches for us and prays that we do not perish in the storm.

After the first fright, when they see him walking on the water—it is comforting to see that even such "proper men" as these fishermen from Galilee "cried out in fear"—Peter wants to imitate Jesus right away and dares to go out on the water, toward Jesus. A strong image for the hazardous business of faith, which makes possible the seemingly impossible, simply through trust in Jesus' call: Come! Dare to do it, do not fear! And how comforting it is to us that Peter experiences this: If I rely only on my own strength, I will perish. If I look to Jesus and his hand grabs hold of me, I will not perish. Thank you, Peter; you give me the courage to dare to believe!

The Gospel of Matthew 15:21–28

And Jesus went away from there and withdrew to the district of Tyre and Sidon. And behold, a Canaanite woman from that region came out and cried, "Have mercy on me, O Lord, Son of David; my daughter is severely possessed by a demon." But he did not answer her a word. And his disciples came and begged him, saying, "Send her away, for she is crying after us." He answered, "I was sent only to the lost sheep of the house of Israel." But she came and knelt before him, saying, "Lord, help me." And he answered, "It is not fair to take the children's bread and throw it to the dogs." She said, "Yes, Lord, yet even the dogs eat the crumbs that fall from their masters' table." Then Jesus answered her, "O woman, great is your faith! Let it be done for you as you desire." And her daughter was healed instantly.

à

Two Types of Mercy

You have to imagine the scene vividly: Jesus withdraws with his followers to the neighboring heathen coastal area, to the district of Tyre and Sidon. As Jews they are foreigners there, so they wish to conduct themselves as quietly and inconspicuously as possible. Jesus' reputation is, of course, already well known, even abroad. His healings are discussed everywhere, for where are there no ill people?

The time of remaining hidden is over! A woman somehow finds out who he is, this stranger with his people. She seeks him out and begins to beg loudly for help, not for herself, but for her suffering-plagued daughter. That she thinks a demon is tormenting her child can be understood by every mother who must stand by and watch as her own child falls into the clutches of evil.

Distressing, this mother's call for help: "Have mercy on me!" And astonishing, that she, although she is not of the Jewish religion, nevertheless addresses Jesus as the Son of David, from whom the Jews await deliverance and salvation.

Even more shocking is the behavior of Jesus. He does not answer her with a single word. It seems that he does not even notice her. Is this the mercy he himself preaches? His disciples seem much more compassionate here. They plead for the woman, whose need has affected them. Of course, another motive then comes to light, which is less pure. It is obviously embarrassing to the companions of Jesus that this woman is making such a commotion, that she will not let Jesus "rid" himself of her, and that she continues her cries for help, which, in the meantime, have probably already led to a whole crowd of curious onlookers.

Jesus' compassion is of another kind. He does not immediately grant what is requested just to have peace, like parents who cannot endure the persistent "pestering" of their children and buy them whatever they want. Jesus sets a clear limit: His mission applies to his own people, the Jews, and not to foreigners! But the woman will not let up; she throws herself in his path and makes the heart-rending plea: Help me!

It is incomprehensible that Jesus does not allow himself to be moved. His hardness appalls us. He calls his people "children" and the heathens "dogs", he who constantly preaches brotherly love. How do these things go together? The outcome proves him right. The heathen woman takes his words and turns them around: Yes, bread is for the children first, but the little dogs nevertheless get whatever falls under the table.

Now Jesus is moved. This strong, unshakable faith moves him. For this woman has clearly shown him that she knows: I have no right to your help, but I do have a confidence that is greater than all obstacles. Jesus has placed this woman's faith before our eyes for all time. But first he gives it a proper challenge through his apparent harshness and brings it to fruition. The quick compassion of the disciples, when compared with that, turns out to be cheap convenience that seeks only its own peace.

TWENTY-FIRST SUNDAY IN ORDINARY TIME

The Gospel of Matthew 16:13–20

Now when Jesus came into the district of Caesarea Philippi, he asked his disciples, "Who do men say that the Son of man is?" And they said, "Some say John the Baptist, others say Elijah, and others Jeremiah or one of the prophets." He said to them, "But who do you say that I am?" Simon Peter replied, "You are the Christ, the Son of the living God." And Jesus answered him, "Blessed are you, Simon Bar-Jona! For flesh and blood has not revealed this to you, but my Father who is in heaven. And I tell you, you are Peter, and on this rock I will build my Church, and the gates of Hades shall not prevail against it. I will give you the keys of the kingdom of heaven, and whatever you bind on earth shall be bound in heaven, and whatever you loose on earth shall be loosed in heaven." Then he strictly charged the disciples to tell no one that he was the Christ.

&

On This Rock

Let us go in spirit to the place where the scene of today's Gospel is playing, to the north of Galilee, to that high rock face from whose foot one of the richly flowing sources of the Jordan streams. Anyone who reads this Gospel in that place understands why it was here, of all places, that Jesus gave Simon the name of Peter, the rock.

Time and place are significant here. It is the northernmost boundary of the Holy Land.

Jesus withdraws with the apostles to this place. He is standing at a turning point, and his own, the apostles, are to carry it out with him. Up to this point, his public work has been highly successful. Ever greater crowds are coming from afar to hear him, to touch him, to ask for healing and help. The enmity against him, however, is also becoming ever clearer: He is a blasphemer, a lawbreaker, according to the deadly accusations. And the road he will take from this turning point on is emerging with ever greater clarity: to Jerusalem, into suffering, onto the Cross.

In this hour, Jesus wants to clarify who he really is. Not for the sake of some "personality cult", not to draw attention to himself as a "guru", but in order to prepare them for what will happen in Jerusalem and what they will find so difficult to comprehend: his death on the Cross. So first he asks about the opinion people have of him. The various views have one thing in common: People somehow feel that he is a man of God. "But you", he asks further, "who do you say that I am?"

Peter's response has become the confession of faith of Christians for all time, the rock on which Christianity is built, on which it stands or falls: "You are the Messiah, the Christ, the Son of the living God." Over this confession minds will part ways time and again: Is Jesus one of the greatest religious figures of human history, or is he the Son of God incarnate, true God and true man?

Before the high rock cliff near Caesarea Philippi, what has since formed the rock-solid foundation of the Christian faith is clearly pronounced for the first time in plain language.

But then Jesus immediately makes clear: "Simon, son of your father Jona, you do not have this of your own accord" ("flesh and blood"); it is not in your power to comprehend this; God my Father has laid this in your heart. For it exceeds human understanding that a man, Jesus of Nazareth, could truly be God in human form, God's Son incarnate. But that Peter is not talking nonsense with this confession, Jesus proves through words that have turned out to be durable and true for two thousand years now: You are Peter, and on this rock I will build my Church. If this concerned only Peter and his successors to this day, the Church would long since have come to an end. But Jesus promises that he himself will build his Church on Peter and his foundation of faith. And the Lord has kept his word thus far; the gates of hell have not devoured the Church. Often declared dead, she lives, and the old, ill Pope [John Paul II] has shown an astonished world that Jesus' promise to his Church is as powerfully alive as ever.

Twenty-Second Sunday in Ordinary Time

The Gospel of Matthew 16:21–27

From that time Jesus began to show his disciples that he must go to Jerusalem and suffer many things from the elders and chief priests and scribes, and be killed, and on the third day be raised. And Peter took him and began to rebuke him, saying, "God forbid, Lord! This shall never happen to you." But he turned and said to Peter, "Get behind me, Satan! You are a hindrance to me; for you are not on the side of God, but of men."

Then Jesus told his disciples, "If any man would come after me, let him deny himself and take up his cross and follow me. For whoever would save his life will lose it, and whoever loses his life for my sake will find it. For what will it profit a man, if he gains the whole world and forfeits his life? Or what shall a man give in return for his life? For the Son of man is to come with his angels in the glory of his Father, and then he will repay every man for what he has done."

❧

Behind Me, You Satan!

Can one imagine a greater contrast? Peter has just solemnly confessed that Jesus is the Messiah, the Son of the living God, the longed-for Messiah, the long awaited, hoped-for

Savior of God's people from all bondage and oppression. We can sense the joyful enthusiasm with which Peter pronounced this, so to speak, as the voice of the suffering Jewish people.

And then Jesus begins to talk about something completely different: not of victory and new freedom, but of imminent suffering and being killed. That must have seemed like an unbearable contradiction to the apostles and to Peter, above all. How could Jesus be the Savior if he is killed? How is he to be the one who liberates the people from their endless suffering if he himself is to face much suffering?

So it is all too understandable, indeed, likeable in human terms, that Peter immediately wants to act upon the assignment he has just received from Jesus: Never! God forbid that this should happen to you! The Messiah, the Savior, is to conquer, not suffer; he is to liberate, not perish. Peter wants to preserve Jesus from his fate of suffering, and that is why he places himself protectively in front of him.

There is hardly any other passage where Jesus reacts so abruptly and harshly as he does in this moment: "Away with you, behind me, you Satan!" (That is how this must be translated literally.) Peter—a Satan? The Peter whom Jesus made the rock of the Church just a while back? It must strike Jesus deep within his heart that Peter wants to keep him from his path. You want to cause my downfall. He calls him Satan, because Satan did exactly that when he tempted him in the desert, when he wanted to put him off his path.

But unlike his treatment of the devil, Jesus does not drive Peter away; instead, he issues a firm challenge to him. Get behind me again; follow me, because your way is not God's way; your ideas of freedom, happiness, and salvation are not God's plans; they are what men understand by those things.

I can sympathize with Peter. He means well for his beloved Master, not wanting to see him suffer. But the matter is too serious for Jesus simply to let Peter and all who want to be his disciples get away with it. What a profound change of thinking is demanded of us here! Everything rightly resists sorrow and the cross. We are created for happiness and not for the cross. But Jesus knows of a deep, true law of life, without which there is no happiness. It is called: self-denial! He who desires self-realization on his own terms will waste his life. He who risks, gives away, does not anxiously hold on to his life, will gain it. Jesus traveled this road to the end, he pledged his life for us, even for his enemies. In this way, the Cross became a symbol of hope. Peter changed his ways and followed Jesus, even to death on the Cross, which he suffered in Nero's Circus, the place where the Basilica of Saint Peter stands today, where today [2002] his successor Pope John Paul II lives out for us an example of the strength that proceeds from suffering and the cross and also an example of the hope and the courage to face life, which his readiness to suffer radiates.

Matthew 18:15–20

"If your brother sins against you, go and tell him his fault, between you and him alone. If he listens to you, you have gained your brother. But if he does not listen, take one or two others along with you, that every word may be confirmed by the evidence of two or three witnesses. If he refuses to listen to them, tell it to the Church; and if he refuses to listen even to the Church, let him be to you as a Gentile and a tax collector. Truly, I say to you, whatever you bind on earth shall be bound in heaven, and whatever you loose on earth shall be loosed in heaven. Again I say to you, if two of you agree on earth about anything they ask, it will be done for them by my Father in heaven. For where two or three are gathered in my name, there am I in the midst of them."

❧

Tell Me My Faults!

Should you interfere? Should you point out others' faults to them? Should you not rather put your own house in order? Today's Gospel is about dealing properly with the faults of others. Jesus gives his disciples very practical rules for resolving conflict. They are as relevant as ever. For there will always be faults as long as we are fallible human beings.

Jesus is talking about sinning. Thus, he means, not simply harmless faults and weaknesses, but violations of God's commandments, violations against what is good and right. He is addressing dangerous behavior that can bring about great damage. Should I stand by and watch as another person endangers himself and those around him through moral transgressions? But, then, who am I to judge the conduct of the other person? Did Jesus not say: "Judge not, that you be not judged" (Mt 7:1)?

No, we should not judge or condemn; we should, however, tell others their faults. And indeed, not in front of everyone else, but only in person, in private, so as not to expose the other person and force him into a position of self-defense. What do we do instead of this? We talk with everyone we can about the faults of the other person, just not with that person himself. This "backbiting" is almost a national pastime for us. The person affected is often the last to find out that his faults are being discussed. We should talk, not *about* faults, but, rather, *with* the one at fault. And that takes courage, straightforwardness, and a full helping of genuine brotherly love. In front of others, we should rather cover up and keep secret the faults of our neighbor. With him, however, we should discuss them openly. Gossiping is unmerciful; telling someone his faults in private is merciful. If the confidential discussion is successful, then it is a victory of brotherly love; the other person can mend his ways and has not lost face.

If it is not successful, one or two others should join the effort in order to have a serious talk with the guilty party. If this does not help either, then it might become necessary for the congregation, the Church, to part company with the brother, with the sister. For Jesus has given the Church the responsibility "to bind and to loose".

When the Church does this, some like to make the accusation against her that she is unmerciful, that she is exclusionary. But is it more merciful to leave the other person in his faults and not point out to him the dangers of his wrong ways? Should we not be thankful ourselves when others have the courage and loving-kindness to tell us our faults directly and to refrain from whispering about them behind our backs?

Sometimes a seemingly harsh measure, a painful act of separation, is a better aid in bringing someone to his senses and back into the fold than the seeming kindheartedness of looking away and letting him go his own way.

The unanimity that Jesus articulates in the Gospel can grow only where the courage exists to point out each other's faults in a brotherly give-and-take. Where such harmony exists, communal prayer also becomes a mighty help. Nothing, however, brings us together more than this mutual, patient, love-filled assistance in recognizing our own individual faults and overcoming them. God dwells in such a community; there Jesus is in the midst of us.

The Gospel of Matthew 18:21–35

Then Peter came up and said to him, "Lord, how often shall my brother sin against me, and I forgive him? As many as seven times?" Jesus said to him, "I do not say to you seven times, but seventy times seven.

"Therefore the kingdom of heaven may be compared to a king who wished to settle accounts with his servants. When he began the reckoning, one was brought to him who owed him ten thousand talents; and as he could not pay, his lord ordered him to be sold, with his wife and children and all that he had, and payment to be made. So the servant fell on his knees, imploring him, 'Lord, have patience with me, and I will pay you everything.' And out of pity for him the lord of that servant released him and forgave him the debt. But that same servant, as he went out, came upon one of his fellow servants who owed him a hundred denarii; and seizing him by the throat he said, 'Pay what you owe.' So his fellow servant fell down and pleaded with him, 'Have patience with me, and I will pay you.' He refused and went and put him in prison till he should pay the debt. When his fellow servants saw what had taken place, they were greatly distressed, and they went and reported to their lord all that had taken place. Then his lord summoned him and said to him, 'You wicked servant! I forgave you all that debt because you pleaded with me; and should not you have had mercy on your fellow servant, as I had mercy on you?' And in anger his lord delivered him to the jailers, till he should pay all his

debt. So also my heavenly Father will do to every one of you, if you do not forgive your brother from your heart."

୧�

How Difficult Is Forgiving?

If we are to reprove one another—Jesus previously spoke about this in the Gospel—then we must certainly forgive one other as well. But how often? Peter wants to know. On our own, we reach limits. Should I forgive seven times? Even that is quite often and quite difficult. Everything must have an end at some point, forgiving as well.

Now if you want to draw limits to forgiving, Jesus replies, then God will also limit his mercy. Beyond this limit, only God's judgment remains, and none of you can successfully stand before his judgment. In order to make this clear to us, Jesus tells a drastic parable.

One man owes ten thousand talents, which is one hundred million denarii, a million times as much as his fellow servant owes him. On the one hand, a never-payable mountain of debts and, on the other, the small matter of one hundred denarii. Both of them implore the creditor for an extension of their debt; both of them promise to pay everything back. But the one man is in a completely hopeless situation because he will never be able to pay his debt. With some patience, the other man will easily be able to pay back his small sum.

Jesus tells the story in such a way that anger and outrage truly arise in us over the debtor whom the king, in an incomprehensibly magnanimous act of mercy, simply releases from his entire debt. How can he already have forgotten all that in the next moment, treating his fellow servant with such utter inhumanity and brutality exactly at the point where he has just experienced kindness in incomparably greater measure?

It is therefore a question of forgiving. What, after all, is the debt that we have to settle with one another compared to our state of guilt before God? If God is so infinitely generous with us, then should we not let go of the petty scores we have with one another and forgive each other?

The parable, of course, has a catch. More often than not, I feel the insult done to me more painfully than my guilt before God. The wrong done to me does hurt, whether at work, in relationships, or wherever. It sticks deep in my memory and rises to the surface again and again. My ingratitude to God, however, I hardly notice, and that is why I also think about it so little. As with the debtor in this parable, so it is with me: The colleague who has committed some minor malicious act against me, him I see; to avenge myself against him suggests itself to me because I can grab hold of him. The record of debt that I have with God is, by comparison, invisible; it seems to be far away; the day of reckoning lies somewhere in the distant future, so we believe.

It is precisely against this deception that Jesus directs his parable. Think about it: If God wanted to settle scores with you as exactly as you have with your colleague, then your own account of debts would look frightening. How do I get out of this self-deception? There is only one way out: Forgive your brother from your heart. Not just one time or seven times, but time and time again. And you will be amazed to discover that you feel peace and cheerfulness in your heart. You will thankfully begin to understand that God is infinitely kinder to you than you ever were to your colleague.

The Gospel of Matthew 20:1–16a

"For the kingdom of heaven is like a householder who
went out early in the morning to hire laborers for his vineyard. After agreeing with the laborers for a denarius a day,
he sent them into his vineyard. And going out about the
third hour he saw others standing idle in the market place;
and to them he said, 'You go into the vineyard too, and
whatever is right I will give you.' So they went. Going
out again about the sixth hour and the ninth hour, he did
the same. And about the eleventh hour he went out and
found others standing; and he said to them, 'Why do you
stand here idle all day?' They said to him, 'Because no
one has hired us.' He said to them, 'You go into the vineyard too.' And when evening came, the owner of the vineyard said to his steward, 'Call the laborers and pay them
their wages, beginning with the last, up to the first.' And
when those hired about the eleventh hour came, each of
them received a denarius. Now when the first came, they
thought they would receive more; but each of them also
received a denarius. And on receiving it they grumbled at
the householder, saying, 'These last worked only one hour,
and you have made them equal to us who have borne the
burden of the day and the scorching heat.' But he replied
to one of them, 'Friend, I am doing you no wrong; did
you not agree with me for a denarius? Take what belongs
to you, and go; I choose to give to this last as I give to
you. Am I not allowed to do what I choose with what

belongs to me? Or do you begrudge my generosity?' So the last will be first, and the first last."

❧

Sharing Another's Joy without Envy

Unemployment was a terrible scourge in Jesus' time as well. Many never got beyond occasional day jobs. Day laborers, they were called, and they can still be found today as well, in Austria, too. The uncertainty of their legal status exposes them to every possible type of exploitation.

The landowner in today's Gospel is a just man. Early in the morning, he enters into an agreement with a number of laborers for the usual day's pay: one denarius. Since the wine harvest requires so many hands, he goes again at nine, at twelve, and at three in the afternoon to the marketplace to find additional laborers. Even at five o'clock in the afternoon, an hour before the workday's end (for night falls quickly in the East), he finds yet a few more whom no one has hired and takes them to work for the short time.

Understandably, the laborers from the first hour, who already have a twelve-hour day behind them, get upset that the last also receive a full day's pay. The landowner could have simply ignored their protest. The patient answer he gives to one of them already says quite a lot about him. He gives the grumblers three reasons for his unusual behavior. No one has been wronged, because the wage agreed on by all has been paid out; he is free to do as he wishes with his money; he can be generous and also give a full day's pay to the late arrivals who have only worked a short time, so that they do not have to go hungry and so that their families also have something to eat. It would also have been fair to give only a small part of the daily wage to those arriving last. If I do more than simple fairness demands, are you envious because of that?

Envy is the ultimate point of the parable. Begrudging the other person what is given to him; comparing, to see whether others receive more, come away better, are given preference. Envy is the downside of the sense of fairness. Jesus even blesses those who hunger and thirst for justice and dedicate themselves to working for it (Mt 5:6).

Envy no longer looks at fairness; it looks at what I see the other person has, which I begrudge him because I do not have it. It is worthwhile to observe the extent to which the weapon of envy is utilized in advertising and, unfortunately, in petty political battles as well. I can easily test my own level of envy: Am I glad when someone else receives something special, is praised, has success, shows talent?

Jesus has one more thing in mind with this parable: Our entire life is like a long workday. Some people are hardworking, orderly, pious, from early on. Others become that way gradually, some only in the last hour. I have had the chance to experience such "laborers of the eleventh hour", who find their way to God after many wrong turns and much wasted life. To them God will also give the full reward, the gift of eternal life, unearned, simply because he is good. Should that annoy me? Should I not be thankful that God called me early on into his vineyard to a meaningful, devout life? Was God not unbelievably kind to me as well?

The Gospel of Matthew 21:28–32

"What do you think? A man had two sons; and he went to the first and said, 'Son, go and work in the vineyard today.' And he answered, 'I will not'; but afterward he repented and went. And he went to the second and said the same; and he answered, 'I go, sir,' but did not go. Which of the two did the will of his father?" They said, "The first." Jesus said to them, "Truly, I say to you, the tax collectors and the harlots go into the kingdom of God before you. For John came to you in the way of righteousness, and you did not believe him, but the tax collectors and the harlots believed him; and even when you saw it, you did not afterward repent and believe him."

ॐ

The Prostitutes Will Enter before You Do

It is all hanging very much in the balance. In Jerusalem, the situation is intensifying. Will Jesus be accepted or rejected? The great crowd of Passover pilgrims is preparing an enthusiastic reception for him; they shout "Hosanna", see in him the Son of David, the Messiah, who is to come in the name of the Lord and liberate Israel.

It is different with the authorities of the Temple and the nation. They have suspected for a long time that he is a blasphemer and an agitator. The decision is becoming unavoidable: for or against him. Is he the Messiah or not? Did God send him or not?

Jesus cannot relieve them of the decision. He does not relieve us of it, either. But he does show them that they must decide: for or against him, for or against God's invitation. And as he so often does, whenever he calls on someone to make a decision, Jesus couches his challenge in the form of parables. Straightaway he tells three, which we will hear today and on the coming two Sundays.

Today's parable is extremely simple. The answer to his question (and the one Jesus expects) is clear to everyone. Did the first or the second son carry out the will of the father? What matters is, not saying Yes, but what you do. The sullen son, who tells the father an unfriendly No but then is sorry to have behaved in such a way and does do the work after all, has clearly lived up to the will of the father better than the "Yes-sayer".

Although the religious authorities did indeed listen devoutly when John the Baptist made the call to change and repentance, they did not, however, change their lives. But the people who went to him in flocks took his words to heart. Luke reports how the tax collectors converted, the soldiers as well. And Jesus, who of course knew this because he himself had gone to John to be baptized by him, adds: Even the prostitutes converted. And so he says what had to work like a provocation: The prostitutes will enter the kingdom of heaven before you do!

Can anyone be surprised, then, that the authorities were furious with him and decided on his death? On which side would I have stood at that time? Would I have rejected him as well? Would I have shouted with the others: He blasphemes God, to the cross with him? This is not a purely theoretical question, because I have to decide today as well, every day anew, whether I am a Yes-sayer and a No-doer or a No-sayer who then says Yes to God's will after all. And Jesus continues to provoke today. We see someone living a dissolute life; he causes a lot of trouble, does not care about God and his commandments. But then, maybe not until right at the end of his earthly days, he is gripped with remorse; he sees what he has done with his life. He makes a full confession and dies reconciled with God (I am not making this story up!)—and this person is to enter paradise before everyone else? Jesus promised exactly that to the one crucified on his right. Is all the trouble to lead an upright life worth it, then? Yes, completely worth it, if I never forget in the process that I am always dependent on God's mercy. And that is what prostitutes often comprehend better.

The Transfiguration of Christ. Icon by Feofan Grek (Theophanes the Greek, late fourteenth century).

Jesus stands, shining with the splendor of divine light, on the peak of Mount Tabor; Elijah and Moses converse with him. The three apostles, blinded, have sunk to the ground; Peter (left) lifts himself up to look at the Lord.

(Second Sunday of Lent, Mt 17:1–9)

The Sermon on the Mount, illumination from the Gospel Book of Otto III (ca. 1000).

Jesus speaks from a chair (typical for a teacher in the Middle Ages). Next to him stand the twelve apostles, below them the rest of the audience.

(Fourth Sunday in Ordinary Time—All Saints, Mt 5:1–12a)

Jesus Walking on the Sea, illustration from the Codex Egberti in Trier (ca. 980).

The wind churns up the sea, but Jesus strides quite calmly over the water. Peter is about to drown; Jesus grabs him and pulls him out of the water.

(Nineteenth Sunday in Ordinary Time, Mt 14:22–33)

III

The Calling of Saint Matthew, by Caravaggio (1599/1600).

The tax collector Matthew is busy with his money. Then Jesus' call and the "divine" light hit him. Peter stands next to Jesus and imitates his gestures.

(Tenth Sunday in Ordinary Time, Mt 9:9–13)

IV

Doubting Thomas, by Caravaggio (1600/1601).

With almost "scientific" thoroughness, Thomas examines the wound in Jesus' side. The others are also interested. The other two apostles both watch the event in silence.

(Second Sunday of Easter, Jn 20:19–31)

V

Pietà by Michelangelo (1499), photograph taken by Robert E. Hupka (1965).

The Mother with her dead Son in her lap is as if left alone with the pain of Golgotha. And yet, the work of the twenty-five-year-old Michelangelo radiates deep joy.

VI

Pietà by Michelangelo, Jesus' face (1499), photograph taken by
Robert E. Hupka (1965).

Michelangelo gave Jesus a countenance that no longer bears
the signs of the scars of Calvary. His body is already beyond
suffering, beyond death.

(Good Friday, the Passion, Jn 19:16–35)

VII

The Paschal Lamb, detail from the Altar of Nicholas of Verdun (1181).

The tomb is open; Jesus climbs forth as the Victor. The Cross is set up to his right as a symbol of victory. The guards are sleeping; one of them is about to wake up. The text around the image, translated, says: "The Paschal Lamb—the Father gave life to him who had lain three days in the tomb."

(Easter, Mt 28:1–10)

VIII

The Gospel of Matthew 21:33–44

"Hear another parable. There was a householder who planted a vineyard, and set a hedge around it, and dug a wine press in it, and built a tower, and leased it to tenants, and went into another country. When the season of fruit drew near, he sent his servants to the tenants, to get his fruit; and the tenants took his servants and beat one, killed another, and stoned another. Again he sent other servants, more than the first; and they did the same to them. Afterward he sent his son to them, saying, 'They will respect my son.' But when the tenants saw the son, they said to themselves, 'This is the heir; come, let us kill him and have his inheritance.' And they took him and cast him out of the vineyard, and killed him. When therefore the owner of the vineyard comes, what will he do to those tenants?" They said to him, "He will put those wretches to a miserable death, and lease the vineyard to other tenants who will give him the fruits in their seasons."

Jesus said to them, "Have you never read in the scriptures:
'The very stone which the builders rejected
has become the head of the corner;
this was the Lord's doing,
and it is marvelous in our eyes'?
Therefore I tell you, the kingdom of God will be taken away from you and given to a nation producing the fruits of it. And he who falls on this stone will be broken to pieces; but when it falls on any one, it will crush him."

ह

The Fruits Count

Seldom does Jesus speak so clearly about his mission and about himself as he does in this parable. His listeners, those who are familiar with the Bible, know what he is saying here: God is the landowner; his vineyard is Israel, the chosen people; the servants he sends out to get his share of the harvest are the prophets of the Old Covenant, God's messengers to his people. His listeners know how it went with the prophets: they were persecuted, rejected, and even killed. People did not want to hear the prophets, because they said things that made them uncomfortable; they called to mind God's commandments; they threatened with God's punishment.

That is how it was with his people. What more could God have done to move them to repentance? Jesus says it clearly: God was still able to play a final "card"; he still had someone they would respect: he sent his own Son to them.

Seldom does Jesus ever so unambiguously say who he truly is: not just one of the prophets sent by God, but God's own Son. And at the same time Jesus makes clear that, with him, God has sent us the one who means everything to him. What if he is rejected as well? What can God still do then for his people?

Jesus' warning is clear: If you kill me, as you are planning, then you will waste the last chance God is giving you. In the parable: Then the vineyard will be taken from you and given to others, and you will be given your rightful punishment.

This is also how the parable has been understood for the most part by Christians: The Jews rejected Jesus, the Son of

God, which is why God took away their inheritance and gave it to Christians. The Church has taken the place of the synagogue.

This interpretation is incorrect for two reasons. In the first place, Jesus did not exactly carry out his threat. When he was nailed to the Cross, he prayed that God his Father might forgive his enemies, "for they know not what they do" (Lk 23:34). Jesus died for his people. They disowned him, but he did not reject them. He came in order to be the Savior of his people, indeed, the Savior of all people.

After all, he taught us to love our enemies. How could we Christians ever believe that Jesus did not love the Jews who were hostile to him? Did he not die for them as well?

Secondly, this dramatic parable of the vineyard tenants also poses a question to Christians, to every single one of them, to me: Have we brought forth good fruits? Can God be satisfied with us? How often have we rejected, persecuted, and not taken seriously those sent by God! Many who were later canonized had to experience persecution and condemnation in their lifetimes, even in the Church. Does Jesus' threat not apply to us as well, that the kingdom of God will be taken away from us and given to other peoples who bring forth the expected fruits, for example, Africans or Asians?

The Gospel of Matthew 22:1–10

And again Jesus spoke to them in parables, saying, "The kingdom of heaven may be compared to a king who gave a marriage feast for his son, and sent his servants to call those who were invited to the marriage feast; but they would not come. Again he sent other servants, saying, 'Tell those who are invited, Behold, I have made ready my dinner, my oxen and my fat calves are killed, and everything is ready; come to the marriage feast.' But they made light of it and went off, one to his farm, another to his business, while the rest seized his servants, treated them shamefully, and killed them. The king was angry, and he sent his troops and destroyed those murderers and burned their city. Then he said to his servants, 'The wedding is ready, but those invited were not worthy. Go therefore to the streets, and invite to the marriage feast as many as you find.' And those servants went out into the streets and gathered all whom they found, both bad and good; so the wedding hall was filled with guests."

Invitation Rejected

Imagine this: An Eastern king arranges an enormous wedding feast for his son, the successor to the throne. All the high and mighty of the kingdom are solemnly invited—and simply do not come. Even after a second summons—"Come, everything is ready"—not only do they not come, but they make it understood that they have more important things to do, their fields, their businesses; moreover, they beat and even kill the servants of the king.

His Eastern listeners must have been outraged at this story. Such crass impoliteness, such disdain of the king—unimaginable and not to be responded to in any way but with the harshest measures. Jesus could be certain that his listeners were completely with him when the king in the story had the city of these noblemen reduced to rubble and ashes. It would be easy to cite examples from our time as well.

Whenever Jesus truly gripped his audience with such a story, the application regularly followed, almost like an attack. *You* conduct yourselves in such a way! *You* are these incomprehensible ingrates! For *you* the king of heaven has prepared the most magnificent wedding feast; he has given his all, so that it will be a unique feast. And you simply have "more important" things to do.

Jesus told this parable—like the two previous parables—shortly before his Passion in Jerusalem: Do you not comprehend then what God is doing for you? Do you not see that he has even sent you his only Son? Why do you not accept his invitation? Why are you so indifferent to God's loving-kindness? Why are you so hostile and filled with hate toward the One he sent, his Son?

The first point of the parable concerns Jesus' struggle with his own, the Jewish people. Because they reject him, as in the parable, the king then invites strangers to the wedding, the other nations, the heathen. That is the primary meaning of the parable, and it is a shocking expression of

Jesus' pain and sorrow over his people and, above all, over their leaders, who did not want to comprehend that he was the Messiah promised by God.

But the parable is also told to us today, and it no longer concerns only the Jewish leaders of Jesus' time. For God's invitation to the marriage feast of his Son is still open today. God has prepared for us, the nations who have received the Christian inheritance, a sumptuous and gift-laden feast. The table is richly set. How many treasures Christianity has prepared for us! Instead of gratefully accepting them, we do not want to come, like those who were invited in the parable. Everything imaginable is more important to us, our business and our free time; we would rather nibble at other religions, search for our satisfaction in esoterica. And bashing the servants of the Church has almost become a matter of course in the meantime.

But Jesus seems to be saying to our old Europe even today: Then I will simply invite strangers to my wedding feast; they will gladly accept the invitation. Will there perhaps be a change of thinking for us as well then? A new joy in the feast of the Christian faith, in Jesus' invitation, which goes out to us Sunday after Sunday, even though at present it is forgotten by many?

Twenty-Ninth Sunday in Ordinary Time

The Gospel of Matthew 22:15–21

Then the Pharisees went and took counsel how to entangle him in his talk. And they sent their disciples to him, along with the Herodians, saying, "Teacher, we know that you are true, and teach the way of God truthfully, and care for no man; for you do not regard the position of men. Tell us, then, what you think. Is it lawful to pay taxes to Caesar, or not?" But Jesus, aware of their malice, said, "Why put me to the test, you hypocrites? Show me the money for the tax." And they brought him a coin. And Jesus said to them, "Whose likeness and inscription is this?" They said, "Caesar's." Then he said to them, "Render therefore to Caesar the things that are Caesar's, and to God the things that are God's."

ॐ

. . . And to God, What Is God's

There are sayings that change the course of history. We hear such a saying today. It decisively shaped the relationship between religion and politics, Church and state, gave it an orientation fundamentally different from that of Islam, for instance. Our modern democratic forms of state are influenced by it: It is Jesus' saying that we should give to Caesar the things that are Caesar's and to God the things that are God's.

Where and when did Jesus utter this decisive saying? In Jerusalem, a few days before his suffering, when various parties were making every attempt to dispose of him. They were seeking a reason to bring about his downfall. The trap they set for him was a genuine catch-22: paying taxes to the emperor (Caesar), to the Roman occupying forces, meant recognizing them as a legitimate power. But the "fundamentalists" among the Jews rejected this. They preferred armed rebellion, assassination attacks on the Romans.

If they were apprehended by the Romans, then they met their end on the cross, like the two criminals who were executed with Jesus.

The Pharisees, who set the trap for Jesus, were for compromise: For the sake of peace you had to pay taxes, but when the Messiah came, then he would free his people from the yoke of the Romans. If Jesus considers himself the Messiah, he must reject paying taxes, they thought. If he does, they can hand him over to the Romans as a rebel. If he does not, then neither is he the promised liberator.

Jesus, who saw through their intent, took hold of them by their hypocrisy: Show the Roman coin! Does it not bear the image and name of the emperor? How is it that you take it in hand when human images are forbidden to the Jews? It belongs to the emperor, so give it to him! Much more important, however, is that you give God what belongs to him.

With these words, Jesus drew the line of separation once and for all between politics and religion, between service of state and service of God. The emperor let himself be worshipped as God; to obey him was divine service. All dictators have attempted to get, not only the money of their

134

subjects, but their souls as well. They have always wanted to have the whole man for themselves. This is what Hitler did, and Stalin was no different. For this reason, every religion, but especially the Church, was a thorn in their side.

For, on the one hand, Jesus instructed his disciples to be obedient to the secular authority, even when it was a foreign ruler like the Roman occupying force. But at the same time, he made it clear that man should worship only God: Give to God the things that are God's! The coins bear the image and inscription of the emperor, so give them to him, because they belong to him. You, however, bear in yourselves the image of God, for man was created in God's image. Therefore, give yourselves, your hearts, your lives, to the One to whom they belong.

Wherever religion and politics are mixed, neither prospers. We have had to learn this painfully in Austria. Do God and religion have no business at all in politics, then? They do, namely, in reminding us that man is more than commerce, money, politics, which are all important and should be properly conducted. But they are only a means, never the meaning and goal of human life.

THIRTIETH SUNDAY IN ORDINARY TIME

The Gospel of Matthew 22:34–40

But when the Pharisees heard that he had silenced the Sadducees, they came together. And one of them, a lawyer, asked him a question, to test him. "Teacher, which is the great commandment in the law?" And he said to him, "You shall love the Lord your God with all your heart, and with all your soul, and with all your mind. This is the great and first commandment. And a second is like it, You shall love your neighbor as yourself. On these two commandments depend all the law and the prophets."

ਡ

And Have Not Love . . .

Again a trick question, again an attempt to set a trap for Jesus, to find a reason to accuse and kill him. The question looks harmless: Which command is the most important? Maybe he will get entangled in the many discussions about the many commandments and prohibitions of the Bible and Jewish tradition—over six hundred have been counted.

Jesus' answer is so simple and clear that even his fiercest adversaries are unable to contradict it. To this day there is no answer more concise or more convincing: Love God completely and your neighbor as yourself. This contains everything God commands; he who keeps and lives both these commandments has fulfilled all the other commandments.

Jesus' answer is so familiar to us, so self-evident after two thousand years of repetition, that we might too quickly pass over the meaning and scope of this double commandment of the love of God and neighbor. For do we truly know what it means to love God with all our heart and our neighbor as well? Jesus says that on these two commandments depend everything we have to do, everything God expects from us.

How peculiar: when people truly live both these commandments, it becomes obvious to all that the only thing that really matters is love. People easily sensed this about good Pope John XXIII or Mother Teresa of Calcutta. But when the issue is that *I* should live and translate that into action, then it looks much more difficult.

In the "song of love" in the First Epistle to the Corinthians (13:1–13), Paul names several characteristics of love: it is patient, kind, does not boast, does not seek its own advantage, does not let itself be provoked to anger, does not bear a grudge when evil is done, takes pleasure, not in wrongdoing but only in the truth, bears all things, hopes all things, withstands all things. If I compare this list with my own conduct, I realize that I am still a long way from the end of my journey and have many battles to fight and perhaps much to suffer before I achieve such a love.

How do I get there? Love, says Saint Augustine, means first of all: I am glad that you exist! It is good that there is a "you"! Love begins with goodwill, and from this it then follows that I also do good to the other person. I have to add here: Am I good to my neighbor? Not just the question of whether I like him. What I spontaneously feel is not within my power. But I can very well wish the other person good, desire his welfare.

And here we understand why Jesus inseparably ties together the love of God and neighbor. To love my neighbor, who of course is not always my favorite person, who on occasion might even be my enemy, who in particular needs my help, there is no surer way than to think about the fact that God is well-disposed toward him. When I take into consideration that God totally loves this neighbor who is so troublesome to me and that he accepts even me with all my faults and says Yes to me, then surely I can try to love my neighbor as well.

In such magnificent people as John XXIII or Mother Teresa, we see the powerful extent to which people who love God with their entire heart, soul, and might are capable of loving their neighbor. And then we understand what Saint Augustine is saying: "Love, and then do what you will!" For you are certainly doing the right thing then.

Thirty-First Sunday in Ordinary Time

The Gospel of Matthew 23:1–12

Then said Jesus to the crowds and to his disciples, "The scribes and the Pharisees sit on Moses' seat; so practice and observe whatever they tell you, but not what they do; for they preach, but do not practice. They bind heavy burdens, hard to bear, and lay them on men's shoulders; but they themselves will not move them with their finger. They do all their deeds to be seen by men; for they make their phylacteries broad and their fringes long, and they love the place of honor at feasts and the best seats in the synagogues, and salutations in the market places, and being called rabbi by men. But you are not to be called rabbi, for you have one teacher, and you are all brethren. And call no man your father on earth, for you have one Father, who is in heaven. Neither be called masters, for you have one master, the Christ. He who is greatest among you shall be your servant; whoever exalts himself will be humbled, and whoever humbles himself will be exalted."

The Best Seats

This Gospel concerns, above all, people in high offices and leading positions, especially in the Church, but also in politics and in other official positions. It is a Gospel that concerns me as a bishop. It frightens and encourages me at the same time. It shows the dangers that lurk in the offices of the Church, and it shows simple ways to avoid these dangers.

He who preaches a lot must especially be on guard that there is not too great a difference between word and deed, between sermon and life. He who teaches a lot must take great care lest he demand from others what he is neither ready nor able to live up to himself.

Anyone who is in a high-profile, high-visibility position is in danger of gradually acquiring an ever-greater taste for being in the spotlight in every place, at every festival, at every religious celebration, and—one must add nowadays—in the media in all its forms.

Jesus does not criticize the fact that there are people who are appointed to preach and to teach or that there are exalted offices and that these are associated with certain positions of honor. What he reproaches the scribes and Pharisees with is their pursuit of recognition, their desire to be seen, their pushing themselves to the fore, and their craving for honor and making a good impression on others.

In a very poor plantation village in Sri Lanka, I was received with unimaginable honors. For days the first visit of a cardinal had been prepared: garlands, the long road neatly and painstakingly covered with fresh sand, flowers, music, everything that these poor people were able to muster. When we finally reached the church—a wretched building—the Jesuit Father, who had been living there, impoverished, for forty years among his parish children, whispered in my ear: "Do not believe that these people did all that on account of Christoph Schönborn. They do it for Christ."

Do not believe you are elevated above others because of your office: "You are all brothers!" The common ground we share in God counts for more than the distinctions in offices and honors: "You have one Father, who is in heaven." Great and small, famous and unknown: we are all children of the one Father.

He who does not forget this will remain simple and modest even in the highest positions. He will understand, above all, that there is only One who is truly great, before whom we are all small, before whom all our differences, which we consider so important, are trivial.

He who keeps this in his heart will not exploit a high office for himself but will view it as a position of service. The only ones who are truly great are those who, even "way up", keep serving and are thus close to their fellowman. I know our Pope to be such a person, which is why I do not shy away from calling him "Holy Father". Anyone who is a servant to such an extent is truly a father to many.

The Gospel of Matthew 25:1–13

"Then the kingdom of heaven shall be compared to ten maidens who took their lamps and went to meet the bridegroom. Five of them were foolish, and five were wise. For when the foolish took their lamps, they took no oil with them; but the wise took flasks of oil with their lamps. As the bridegroom was delayed, they all slumbered and slept. But at midnight there was a cry, 'Behold, the bridegroom! Come out to meet him.' Then all those maidens rose and trimmed their lamps. And the foolish said to the wise, 'Give us some of your oil, for our lamps are going out.' But the wise replied, 'Perhaps there will not be enough for us and for you; go rather to the dealers and buy for yourselves.' And while they went to buy, the bridegroom came, and those who were ready went in with him to the marriage feast; and the door was shut. Afterward the other maidens came also, saying, 'Lord, lord, open to us.' But he replied, 'Truly, I say to you, I do not know you.' Watch therefore, for you know neither the day nor the hour."

༃

So Be Ready!

The three Sundays that yet remain until Advent turn our eyes to the final things of life and the world. Some day we will have to give an account of ourselves. The pilgrimage on earth comes to an end for every individual in the hour of death, for mankind as a whole in the Final Judgment, on "Judgment Day". Not to prepare yourself for this, to be unprepared, is unwise, foolish. The two parables on this and the following Sunday deal with that.

We used to have "bridesmaids" in earlier times as well. They awaited the coming of the groom with the bride. If he was delayed—which was not unusual with the traffic conditions of those times—they had to be able to keep their lamps burning long enough. That is, they had to make provisions. If the bridegroom suddenly came late in the night, it was too late to get supplies. This had to happen earlier, with foresight and wise planning.

The parable has different levels of meaning. First, there is the very simple and practical sense of the virtue of prudence. He who neither plans, thinks ahead, nor is prudent can expect bitter surprises in an emergency. This is just as true for the family budget as it is for a business and even for the state as a whole.

But Jesus obviously has even more in mind. It is about more than just the requisite prudence in the affairs of the world. The image of the wedding banquet is talking about the kingdom of God, the world to come, and it talks about the things we have to do and the things that we have to refrain from doing to keep from losing the eternal life of heaven.

Our life on this earth is a time of preparation. Some day, we do not know when, this will also mean for me: "The bridegroom is coming! Go out to meet him!" For in the hour of death, as we believe, the moment has come for going out to meet God. But then it will be too late to get another supply of oil quickly for my lamp. I must be ready and have made provisions already.

Only *before* my final hour can I do something about it—after that, it is too late. Jesus says this in various parables in order to make us aware of how precious the time is, how we must make good use of it to be "ready at all times".

This also explains a section in this parable that shocks many people. When the foolish "bridesmaids" ask the wise ones: "Give us some of your oil", they receive a curt reply: "Then there will not be enough for us and for you." What has happened to sharing; where has brotherly love gone? Jesus seems to want to say exactly this here: The time for sharing and brotherly love is now, here and today! Anyone who constantly puts it off, who does not provide for it daily, will in the hour of death find it too late to obtain the oil of good deeds quickly.

This is therefore the ultimate point of this parable—and of the next: Be alert, for you know neither the day nor the hour. So live in such a way that you are always ready to die, to go before the face of God.

The Gospel of Matthew 25:14–30

"For it will be as when a man going on a journey called his servants and entrusted to them his property; to one he gave five talents, to another two, to another one, to each according to his ability. Then he went away. He who had received the five talents went at once and traded with them; and he made five talents more. So also, he who had the two talents made two talents more. But he who had received the one talent went and dug in the ground and hid his master's money. Now after a long time the master of those servants came and settled accounts with them. And he who had received the five talents came forward, bringing five talents more, saying, 'Master, you delivered to me five talents; here I have made five talents more.' His master said to him, 'Well done, good and faithful servant; you have been faithful over a little, I will set you over much; enter into the joy of your master.' And he also who had the two talents came forward, saying, 'Master, you delivered to me two talents; here I have made two talents more.' His master said to him, 'Well done, good and faithful servant; you have been faithful over a little, I will set you over much; enter into the joy of your master.' And he also who had received the one talent came forward, saying, 'Master, I knew you to be a hard man, reaping where you did not sow, and gathering where you did not winnow; so I was afraid, and I went and hid your talent in the ground. Here you have what is yours.' But his master answered him, 'You wicked and slothful servant! You knew that I reap where I have not sowed, and gather where I have

*not winnowed? Then you ought to have invested my money
with the bankers, and at my coming I should have received
what was my own with interest. So take the talent from him,
and give it to him who has the ten talents. For to every one
who has will more be given, and he will have abundance;
but from him who has not, even what he has will be taken
away. And cast the worthless servant into the outer darkness, where there will be weeping and gnashing of teeth.' "*

❧

God's Trustees

The parable of the talents has become proverbial. Over the
course of time, the large sum of money, which is what this
unit of measurement is about, turned into talents as we
understand them today: the talents we are given to take on
our journey through life. One nice example, among many,
of the influence the Bible has had on our language.

In Jesus' parable, a well-to-do man entrusts his property
to a few of his servants for the time of his absence. He
expects of them that his assets will not be diminished. And
that is possible only if the assets are invested profitably, if
they are managed well. Two of the three servants do this
with great success. They double their master's money.

The third servant deserves special attention: clearly less gifted
("talented") than the other two, he is put in charge of only
one talent. Jesus points him out, probably to warn us of the
dangers of laziness and carelessness. Why does he let the
talent lie fallow? And why the harsh judgment of him?

The parable presupposes one thing: What we are and what
we have is a gift from God. God has given every man his

146

distinctive "talents". We have received them as trustees. It lies in our hands to make something good of them. "Some day" we will have to account for what we have done with the talents lent to us, in the hour of death, at the latest. That Jesus is thinking here about the Last Judgment is expressed very clearly in his words to the three servants: "Come, enter into the joy of your master", Jesus says to the first two; the third he hands over to the "outer darkness", by which hell is surely meant. Therein lies the seriousness of this parable. It reminds us that it is a matter of our eternal fate. A good or bad end is determined by our own choices.

Jesus does not stop, however, with this warning. He also gives us strong motivation for deciding in favor of the good way. The first two both see the trust of their master as an incentive. They see the large sum of money as a chance to do something creative, sensible, and courageous with it, not out of fear of the "boss", but because they clearly enjoy working to support his business. They identify themselves with his interests, as good employees do.

Jesus surely wants to say this: It is wonderful to be an employee of God. Anyone who sees his own talents as gifts from God will be grateful to him for them and will develop them in accordance with his wishes. And God enjoys it when his gifts blossom through our collaboration. For he desires our happiness. That is why he has entrusted us with his gifts.

The third servant is afraid of his master. He sees only his severity, not his trust. That is why he says to himself: Better to do nothing than to do something wrong. Such an attitude will displease any boss. He will part company with such employees. God wants employees who are enthusiastic and ready for action. They are the ones who further the kingdom of God.

CHRIST THE KING

The Gospel of Matthew 25:31–46

"When the Son of man comes in his glory, and all the angels with him, then he will sit on his glorious throne. Before him will be gathered all the nations, and he will separate them one from another as a shepherd separates the sheep from the goats, and he will place the sheep at his right hand, but the goats at the left. Then the King will say to those at his right hand, 'Come, O blessed of my Father, inherit the kingdom prepared for you from the foundation of the world; for I was hungry and you gave me food, I was thirsty and you gave me drink, I was a stranger and you welcomed me, I was naked and you clothed me, I was sick and you visited me, I was in prison and you came to me.' Then the righteous will answer him, 'Lord, when did we see you hungry and feed you, or thirsty and give you drink? And when did we see you a stranger and welcome you, or naked and clothe you? And when did we see you sick or in prison and visit you?' And the King will answer them, 'Truly, I say to you, as you did it to one of the least of these my brethren, you did it to me.' Then he will say to those at his left hand, 'Depart from me, you cursed, into the eternal fire prepared for the devil and his angels; for I was hungry and you gave me no food, I was thirsty and you gave me no drink, I was a stranger and you did not welcome me, naked and you did not clothe me, sick and in prison and you did not visit me.' Then they also will answer, 'Lord, when did we see you hungry or thirsty or a stranger or naked or sick or in

prison, and did not minister to you?' Then he will answer
them, 'Truly, I say to you, as you did it not to one of the
least of these, you did it not to me.' And they will go
away into eternal punishment, but the righteous into eter-
nal life."

&

Everything Is Decided Today

Michelangelo's *Last Judgment* in the Sistine Chapel in the
Vatican is probably the most famous portrayal of what today's
Gospel is talking about. One day, "when the Son of man
comes in his glory", there will be a final separation, "as a
shepherd separates his sheep from the goats". One day the
final account will be known, plus and minus will stand there
in plain view.

It is God's Final Judgment. But how will it come about?
What standard will be used to measure; which criteria will
be used to judge? Two big surprises:

The Judgment has already taken place. Only at the end
will that which was decided long ago become clear. Everything was decided where we might have expected it too
little or not at all: in the attitude toward my neighbor. How
I ultimately stand before God one day is decided today by
the question of whether I was aware of my ill neighbor and
visited him. Jesus names six instances of need: the hungry,
the thirsty, strangers, the naked, the sick, and those in prison.
They stand for all forms of need and suffering.

And now the second surprising thing: Jesus identifies himself with all of those who suffer such deprivation. Whoever
notices them finds him. Whoever does them good also does

it to him. "When did we see you and help you?" To this amazing question Jesus gives the decisive answer: "As you did it to one of the least of these my brethren, you did it to me."

What counts with God is the love and attention given selflessly and as a matter of course to the neighbor who needs my help. On this, Jesus tells us, your eternal salvation is decided. The decision to do this is made daily, and the important thing is, not whether we are aware of it, but that we do it.

One thing frightens me about Jesus' discussion of the judgment of the world: The "goats" on the left, who are given over to eternal punishment, did not at all realize that they had failed to see God when they did not turn their attention to those suffering need. How easily our neighbor is overlooked! In God's sight, failure to do good weighs more heavily than doing evil. I might comfort myself with the fact that I have not killed anyone. But that is not enough in God's sight if I have nevertheless found no time for the sick, have not noticed the hunger and thirst of my neighbor, have not given shelter to strangers, in short, if I have been unaware of the needy.

Sins of omission should frighten us. For whatever good I have failed to do is irretrievably past. My neighbor, who might have needed me, whom I failed to see (maybe because I was too preoccupied with myself and my wishes), was Jesus himself, who was waiting for me. My God, help me so that I will be able to show in my last hour at least a few moments when I served you in my suffering neighbor.

LENT AND THE EASTER SEASON

The Gospel of Matthew 4:1–11

Then Jesus was led up by the Spirit into the wilderness to be tempted by the devil. And he fasted forty days and forty nights, and afterward he was hungry. And the tempter came and said to him, "If you are the Son of God, command these stones to become loaves of bread." But he answered, "It is written,

'Man shall not live by bread alone,
but by every word that proceeds from the mouth of God.' "

Then the devil took him to the holy city, and set him on the pinnacle of the temple, and said to him, "If you are the Son of God, throw yourself down; for it is written,

'He will give his angels charge of you,'
and

'On their hands they will bear you up,
lest you strike your foot against a stone.' "

Jesus said to him, "Again it is written, 'You shall not tempt the Lord your God.' " Again, the devil took him to a very high mountain, and showed him all the kingdoms of the world and the glory of them; and he said to him, "All these I will give you, if you will fall down and worship me." Then Jesus said to him, "Begone, Satan! for it is written,

'You shall worship the Lord your God
and him only shall you serve.' "

Then the devil left him, and behold, angels came and ministered to him.

The Devil Is Finished

Without a doubt there are such things: the many temptations to which we are all exposed. They can confront us in thousands of forms: the temptation to drive too fast, to eat or drink too much, to say a mocking, disparaging word, to show to others one's own little bit of power, to let it be felt, to exploit it to one's own advantage, to make things better for yourself at someone else's expense, and so on in a multitude of variations. Who does not know them, these temptations and many others, right up to rebellion against God?

The Gospel from the first Sunday of Lent, however, says much more: Someone is behind the temptations to which even Jesus is exposed. The Bible bluntly calls him the devil. He exists, and he is the tempter, who does not like man, who attempts to cause his downfall because he does not want things to go well with him and because he begrudges us our happiness. We have to deal with him in all the battles of our lives; he does not let up; he gives no rest. Unless we conquer him. Jesus shows that this is possible. Let us see how he does it.

The devil takes hold of us by our weak sides. But he always packages his attacks well; he is a master of appearances. He pretends that he has something good for us, for only in this way can he succeed in luring us. After forty days in the desert, Jesus is tempted with three basic needs: the need to have his hunger satisfied, the need to be recognized, and the need to have power. None of these three is in itself bad. Parents have power over their children, not to abuse, but to protect, to raise them, just like the boss with his employees. Jesus also has power. He is, after all, the Son of God. How will he use it? For his own gratification? To gain public success for himself? A leap from the pinnacle of the Temple—that would be a media event that could quickly make him famous! Then he could set himself up as the ruler over all the kingdoms of the world! That would be his role as the Son of God and Messiah, would it not? How will Jesus use his power? How does he respond to the temptations?

Three times Jesus responds to the devil with the word of God. "Man shall not live by bread alone": Food is important to life. Even more important to life is being in agreement with God. "You shall not tempt God": Do not provoke him. Do not do things that you cannot answer for before God! "God only shall you serve": Do not throw yourself down before men; do not idolize anyone, especially the devil.

Jesus resists the devil, and then the devil leaves him. It is therefore possible to conquer the devil. Jesus shows how this is done: He does not let anything dissuade him from God. Through all the temptations, he truly remains the faithful Son of God. We will not always succeed in being faithful. Sometimes we will succumb to temptations. But Jesus faithfully stands by us when we ask for his help. After all, he conquered the tempter for us in the desert. Actually, the devil has been finished ever since.

SECOND SUNDAY OF LENT

———

The Gospel of Matthew 17:1–9

And after six days Jesus took with him Peter and James and John his brother, and led them up a high mountain apart. And he was transfigured before them, and his face shone like the sun, and his garments became white as light. And behold, there appeared to them Moses and Elijah, talking with him. And Peter said to Jesus, "Lord, it is well that we are here; if you wish, I will make three booths here, one for you and one for Moses and one for Elijah." He was still speaking, when behold, a bright cloud overshadowed them, and a voice from the cloud said, "This is my beloved Son, with whom I am well pleased; listen to him." When the disciples heard this, they fell on their faces, and were filled with awe. But Jesus came and touched them, saying, "Rise, and have no fear." And when they lifted up their eyes, they saw no one but Jesus only.

And as they were coming down the mountain, Jesus commanded them, "Tell no one the vision, until the Son of man is raised from the dead."

❧

Unforgettable Hour!

What takes place at that time on a high mountain is one of the unforgettable memories of the three witnesses whom

Jesus takes with him. What they experience there is hard to capture in words. Before their eyes the face of Jesus is transformed; it becomes "shining like the sun"; his garments become blinding, "white as light". They see two figures—they identify them as Moses and Elijah—talking with Jesus, a cloud that envelops them, and a voice that calls Jesus "beloved Son". Then suddenly everything is gone, and they see only Jesus, alone as he was before.

And yet everything is no longer like it was before. This unique event never leaves their minds after they climb down again from the mountain with Jesus. What has happened? What does it mean?

There are experiences you have once and never again forget. I could count off a whole series straightaway, experiences of an incomparable kind, which people have confided to me over the years, which they tell about as shyly and hesitantly as the three apostles told about what they saw and heard on the mountain. "Experiences of God", one could say, "mystical experiences", "hours of grace"—words fail here.

There really are such things, and many more people have probably experienced such unique moments than we assume in the turmoil and rush of our daily life. There may have been experiences of the nearness of God in childhood; experiences of war, where, in the middle of the gray, the light of divine presence shone; intense impressions from nature that let us sense God the Creator; or the look into a good human face in which the love and care of God shines.

What is it, then, that the three experience on the mountain? First of all, this: that Jesus "lights up" before them. For a brief moment, his divine splendor shines through his human exterior, and this sight must have been something unimaginably glorious. That is also why Peter wants this moment to linger and wishes that they could build three booths on the mountain, so that they could hold on to the joy of this hour.

It lies in the nature of these special moments of intense joy, however, that you cannot hold on to them. Daily life comes again; they have to climb down from the mountain of the Transfiguration into the troubles of earthly life, and the road will lead to the hill of Golgotha, to the Cross, the suffering, and the death of Jesus in Jerusalem.

And then another humiliation is added: Later, when the pressure comes and they find themselves in dire straits, then these three forget what they have experienced on the mountain. The same three are there when Jesus suffers mortal fear in the garden of the Mount of Olives and sweats blood— they are sleeping. And when he is arrested, they run away in fear.

Even those of us who might have experienced "hours of grace", "experiences of God", are not therefore immune to such forgetting. When the pressure becomes great, then the memory of what we have experienced fades, the memory that God exists and that he lets us feel his presence, too. And yet: once you have experienced God's presence so clearly, you cannot forget completely. Because God himself stays near. And reminds us.

The Gospel of John 4:5–15, 19–26, 39a, 40–42

So he came to a city of Samaria, called Sychar, near the field that Jacob gave to his son Joseph. Jacob's well was there, and so Jesus, wearied as he was with his journey, sat down beside the well. It was about the sixth hour.

There came a woman of Samaria to draw water. Jesus said to her, "Give me a drink." For his disciples had gone away into the city to buy food. The Samaritan woman said to him, "How is it that you, a Jew, ask a drink of me, a woman of Samaria?" For Jews have no dealings with Samaritans. Jesus answered her, "If you knew the gift of God, and who it is that is saying to you, 'Give me a drink,' you would have asked him, and he would have given you living water." The woman said to him, "Sir, you have nothing to draw with, and the well is deep; where do you get that living water? Are you greater than our father Jacob, who gave us the well, and drank from it himself, and his sons, and his cattle?" Jesus said to her, "Every one who drinks of this water will thirst again, but whoever drinks of the water that I shall give him will never thirst; the water that I shall give him will become in him a spring of water welling up to eternal life." The woman said to him, "Sir, give me this water, that I may not thirst, nor come here to draw." . . .

The woman said to him, "Sir, I perceive that you are a prophet. Our fathers worshiped on this mountain; and you say that in Jerusalem is the place where men ought to worship." Jesus said to her, "Woman, believe me, the hour

*is coming when neither on this mountain nor in Jerusalem
will you worship the Father. You worship what you do not
know; we worship what we know, for salvation is from the
Jews. But the hour is coming, and now is, when the true
worshipers will worship the Father in spirit and truth, for
such the Father seeks to worship him. God is spirit, and
those who worship him must worship in spirit and truth."
The woman said to him, "I know that Messiah is coming
(he who is called Christ); when he comes, he will show us
all things." Jesus said to her, "I who speak to you am
he." . . .*

*Many Samaritans from that city believed in him. . . .
So when the Samaritans came to him, they asked him to
stay with them; and he stayed there two days. And many
more believed because of his word. They said to the woman,
"It is no longer because of your words that we believe, for
we have heard for ourselves, and we know that this is
indeed the Savior of the world."*

(Complete text: Jn 4:5–42)

&

Give Me a Drink

For three Sundays in Lent, there are especially long Gospels.
One should read them in their entirety. They are three stories of deliverance: Jesus and the Samaritan woman; Jesus
and the man born blind; Jesus and his deceased friend Lazarus. A woman finds her way out of the dead ends of her
life. A blind man receives sight. Jesus calls a dead man back
to life. These deliverances are recounted during Lent because
they prove what is said by the people at the end of today's

Gospel: Jesus is "indeed the Savior of the world". How do they arrive at this conviction?

Jesus sits down beside Jacob's well, weary from the long journey (on foot!) in the midday heat. Nobody goes to the well at this hour. Early in the morning when it is still cool, or in the evening when it cools down again, the women come with their water jugs, which they carry on their heads. One, however, comes alone in the sweltering heat, "around the sixth hour", at noon. She is certain she will not meet any of the women from the village. For she is ashamed and fears the gossip about her way of life. She has already been married five times, and now she is living with a sixth man. Jesus will later tell her this outright. But first he surprises her. No trace of contempt or reproach. Just a request: "Give me a drink!"

All of this is unusual for the times: A Jewish man asks a Samaritan—even though she is a stranger and a woman! And that opens her heart: someone who does not condemn her. Who is this thirsty wanderer who simply asks her for water? And so a conversation begins. He speaks to her about a water that he can give. She hopes, misunderstanding him, no longer to have to make the arduous walk to the well. He is talking about a different water, an inner spring that needs to be found, which can quench the life-thirst that has driven this woman from one man to another without ever really having that thirst for love and recognition and security satisfied. Jesus promises a spring that never leaves one thirsty again. He arouses her curiosity. The many disappointments she has experienced in her relationships make room for a new hope.

There must have been something unique in the encounter with Jesus. In it, this woman meets someone who sees her completely as she is, neither in order "to have" her nor to criticize, to judge her. This enables her to blossom, to see that she has been on the wrong path for a long time and that there is someone who can satisfy her deep longing, who will not disappoint her one more time. She has found the spring that is able to still her thirst: faith in Jesus. And that inner connection to God, which Jesus calls "worship in spirit and truth".

Since that midday hour at Jacob's well, countless people have had similar experiences in the encounter with Jesus and have found the spring that bubbles up in their hearts, inexhaustible: faith.

And they, like the woman at Jacob's well, have told others about their faith and aroused in them the curiosity to set out for this spring themselves and to draw from it and experience for themselves that Jesus is "indeed the Savior of the world".

"Give me a drink"—is this not what God asks of us all, that we believe him? So that he can satisfy our thirst!

FOURTH SUNDAY OF LENT

———

The Gospel of John 9:1, 6–9, 13–17, 34–38

As he passed by, he saw a man blind from his birth. . . . As he said this, he spat on the ground and made clay of the spittle and anointed the man's eyes with the clay, saying to him, "Go, wash in the pool of Siloam" (which means Sent). So he went and washed and came back seeing. The neighbors and those who had seen him before as a beggar, said, "Is not this the man who used to sit and beg?" Some said, "It is he"; others said, "No, but he is like him." He said, "I am the man.". . .

They brought to the Pharisees the man who had formerly been blind. Now it was a sabbath day when Jesus made the clay and opened his eyes. The Pharisees again asked him how he had received his sight. And he said to them, "He put clay on my eyes, and I washed, and I see." Some of the Pharisees said, "This man is not from God, for he does not keep the sabbath." But others said, "How can a man who is a sinner do such signs?" There was a division among them. So they again said to the blind man, "What do you say about him, since he has opened your eyes?" He said, "He is a prophet.". . .

They answered him, "You were born in utter sin, and would you teach us?" And they cast him out.

Jesus heard that they had cast him out, and having found him he said, "Do you believe in the Son of man?" He answered, "And who is he, sir, that I may believe in him?" Jesus said to him, "You have seen him, and it is he who speaks to you." He said, "Lord, I believe"; and he worshiped him.

(Complete text: Jn 9:1–41)

☙

Seeing or Blind?

Around the world at Easter, numerous adults will receive baptism; in quite a few countries, there are many thousands. Here, where mostly children are baptized, this number is still quite small, but it is growing from year to year.

If you ask the adult baptismal candidates about their personal journey to faith, then you will repeatedly hear stories that are not unlike today's Gospel. Their journey to faith and to baptism is like that of the man born blind to whom Jesus gave the eyesight he had lacked from birth. They experience the transition to faith as a journey to light. In early Christian times, baptism was described as "enlightenment". And that is why today's Gospel was then and is still read as a step in the preparation for baptism.

For this reason I recommend reading in your own Bible all of this very long ninth chapter of John's Gospel; for reasons of space, only an excerpt could be printed here. Whoever reads the story in its entirety can hardly escape the drama of the event. At the beginning there is the miraculous healing of the blind man by Jesus. Several times Jesus gave sight to the blind, and in the lives of the saints, as well, there are again and again reports of the blind being healed, by Padre Pio, for instance.

People begin to ask: What happened, and how did it happen? Who, then, is this man Jesus who healed you? And again and again, the man who was healed tells what Jesus did and how he has received his sight. And in the process he learns: The more often he talks about it, the more clearly he sees for himself who has healed him and what has been given to him. More and more the healed man becomes a believer.

An important element on this journey is of course the resistance he encounters. The "Pharisees" do not want to believe him; they swear at him and finally throw him out. They consider Jesus to be a lawbreaker who cannot be from God. The man who was healed, however, cannot and will not deny what was given to him. He grows because of this hostile rejection; he becomes clearer in his conviction that Jesus is a prophet, yes, even more, the Son of God. He finds his way to full faith in him and worships him.

In this respect, the healed blind man is a model for the journey to faith.

To the degree that I pass on the story of my journey in the faith, my faith becomes firmer, and wherever it proves itself, even against contradiction and resistance, it becomes deeper and more alive and finally leads, as in today's Gospel, to a full encounter with Jesus Christ.

FIFTH SUNDAY OF LENT

The Gospel of John 11:3–7, 17, 20–27, 33b–45

So the sisters sent to him, saying, "Lord, he whom you love is ill." But when Jesus heard it he said, "This illness is not unto death; it is for the glory of God, so that the Son of God may be glorified by means of it."

Now Jesus loved Martha and her sister and Lazarus. So when he heard that he was ill, he stayed two days longer in the place where he was. Then after this he said to the disciples, "Let us go into Judea again."...

Now when Jesus came, he found that Lazarus had already been in the tomb four days.... When Martha heard that Jesus was coming, she went and met him, while Mary sat in the house. Martha said to Jesus, "Lord, if you had been here, my brother would not have died. And even now I know that whatever you ask from God, God will give you." Jesus said to her, "Your brother will rise again." Martha said to him, "I know that he will rise again in the resurrection at the last day." Jesus said to her, "I am the resurrection and the life; he who believes in me, though he die, yet shall he live, and whoever lives and believes in me shall never die. Do you believe this?" She said to him, "Yes, Lord; I believe that you are the Christ, the Son of God, he who is coming into the world."...

[Jesus] was deeply moved in spirit and troubled; and he said, "Where have you laid him?" They said to him, "Lord, come and see." Jesus wept. So the Jews said, "See how he loved him!" But some of them said, "Could not

he who opened the eyes of the blind man have kept this man from dying?"

Then Jesus, deeply moved again, came to the tomb; it was a cave, and a stone lay upon it. Jesus said, "Take away the stone." Martha, the sister of the dead man, said to him, "Lord, by this time there will be an odor, for he has been dead four days." Jesus said to her, "Did I not tell you that if you would believe you would see the glory of God?" So they took away the stone. And Jesus lifted up his eyes and said, "Father, I thank you that you have heard me. I knew that you always hear me, but I have said this on account of the people standing by, that they may believe that you did send me." When he had said this, he cried with a loud voice, "Lazarus, come out." The dead man came out, his hands and feet bound with bandages, and his face wrapped with a cloth. Jesus said to them, "Unbind him, and let him go."

Many of the Jews therefore, who had come with Mary and had seen what he did, believed in him.

(Complete text: Jn 11:1–45)

🙢

Lazarus, Come Out!

Bethany is located near Jerusalem. Three siblings who are especially important to Jesus live there: Mary, Martha, and Lazarus. Jesus stops at their house from time to time and clearly enjoys being with them, feels safe there. But can we speak of Jesus in this way? Does he, God's Son, have such human needs of friendship and security?

Today's Gospel confirms exactly that. Here it becomes quite evident that Jesus loves these three siblings dearly: "See how he loved him!" the people say when they see Jesus weeping bitterly at the tomb. A simple observation comes involuntarily to mind: Jesus had friends. He, the Son of God, truly and completely became man. In that final period right before Easter, when the hostility toward him became ever clearer and his death loomed already on the horizon, his friends in Bethany were obviously especially important to him.

We know from the two thousand years since then that many people have experienced the friendship of Jesus, even though since Easter he no longer comes as a visible guest. The simple prayer at the dinner table, which is well known to many: "Come, Lord Jesus and be our guest . . ." speaks to this experience as well.

But why does Jesus wait so long when someone brings him the news: "Lord, your friend is ill"? Do you not immediately go to your friend when he is deathly ill? Why does he do this to the two sisters, who beg him to come quickly?

I believe that this is also something many people have experienced, much like Mary and Martha. You pray, you implore God for help, and the answer fails to appear: "If you had been here, my brother would not have died", Martha says, when Jesus finally comes—and it is all too late. I know people who have lost their trust in God because, despite all their praying, a dear one died anyway.

It is, of course, a comfort to believe that there will be life after death. Martha believes this when she says: "I know that he will rise again in the resurrection at the last day." And of course, we all know that we must die some day. How often it happens, though, that death comes too soon!

And the death of the beloved brother and friend Lazarus certainly came, seen in human terms, much too soon. Into the grief and pain Jesus says a word that Martha and Mary and many people since then have been able to hold onto whenever sorrow becomes overwhelming: "I am the resurrection and the life; he who believes in me, though he die, yet shall he live." There is a life that does not have to fear even death. Jesus says of himself that he is this life. Whoever follows him, whoever trusts him, does not await the earthly end of life in panic and does not fall through the gate of death into the abyss of nothingness; rather, he enters into full, complete life.

And so that we can trust that faith in Jesus really gives life, Jesus calls his friend, who has been dead for four days, out of the tomb. I firmly believe that Jesus truly raised a dead man, not one who appeared to be dead, at that time. Similar things have been done by saints very often since then. But I also hear in this mighty "Lazarus, come out" a call to me to come out of my tomb and my shackles.

So many fears weigh on my life like a tombstone. Faith lifts them away, loosens the bandages, and lets me live again. I, too, can be Lazarus, someone Jesus calls forth and restores to life.

PALM SUNDAY

The Gospel of Matthew 21:1–11

And when they drew near to Jerusalem and came to Bethphage, to the Mount of Olives, then Jesus sent two disciples, saying to them, "Go into the village opposite you, and immediately you will find a donkey tied, and a colt with her; untie them and bring them to me. If any one says anything to you, you shall say, 'The Lord has need of them,' and he will send them immediately." This took place to fulfil what was spoken by the prophet, saying,

"Tell the daughter of Zion,
Behold, your king is coming to you,
humble, and mounted on a donkey,
and on a colt, the foal of a donkey."

The disciples went and did as Jesus had directed them; they brought the donkey and the colt, and put their garments on them, and he sat on them. Most of the crowd spread their garments on the road, and others cut branches from the trees and spread them on the road. And the crowds that went before him and that followed him shouted, "Hosanna to the Son of David! Blessed is he who comes in the name of the Lord! Hosanna in the highest!" And when he entered Jerusalem, all the city was stirred, saying, "Who is this?" And the crowds said, "This is the prophet Jesus from Nazareth of Galilee."

Sorrow and Easter Joy

Palm Sunday, pussy willows, palm processions: To this day, what began with a great mass of people has remained a popular tradition: the entry of Jesus into Jerusalem. A few days later, a crowd of people will shout to him again, not with the enthusiastic "Hosanna", of course, but with an agitated "to the cross with him!"

Since that dramatic week in Jerusalem approximately in the year 30, Christians everywhere have celebrated its memory. In German, it is called *Kar* Week, from the Old High German *kara*, which means, "worry", "trouble". The English word "care" (still familiar to many from "care packages") has the same origin. Full of trouble and worry are the events that lead to Jesus' arrest, sentencing, and cruel crucifixion, in the end. But everything begins at first so promisingly, and, despite the tragedy of the coming days, everything will ultimately end, not in hopelessness, but with Easter morning.

Let us recall the scene. Jesus goes up to Jerusalem to the Easter feast. Many thousands of pilgrims are on the move in those days. They all want to celebrate Passover, the Jewish Easter feast, in completely overcrowded Jerusalem. In that year there is high tension. The Roman occupying army is on high alert. For in the Jewish faith, the appearance of the Messiah, the great liberator, is awaited at Easter. Many have been asking themselves that year: Could this Jesus of Nazareth be the one we have longed for?

When Jesus is close to the Holy City of Jerusalem, he adds fuel to the fire of this hope: he mounts a female donkey and rides it toward the city. He does this quite consciously, for an ancient prophet had foretold such a thing: The Messiah-king will not come with might and pomp and high on a steed, but humbly and modestly on a donkey, the animal the little people use for riding.

That is exactly how he indicates that he is the Messiah, the awaited king. The people cheer him as the "Son of David", as the descendant of that great king whose mighty inheritance he, they hope, will restore. "Hosanna", they shout, which means "help"—may God stand by the coming king.

It all happened quite differently. After a few days, on Good Friday (*Karfreitag*), Jesus hung on the Cross; in mockery Pilate had "The King of the Jews" written over it. And there was no trace of God sending help to his chosen one. It looked like the end of it all when Jesus lay in the tomb. But it was not the end. Then came Easter morning, the empty tomb, the Resurrected One, the hallelujah.

Christians all over the world will take this dramatic journey with Christ in the coming days. It is called "Holy Week", the high point of all Christian festivals. And whoever joins in celebrating these days and their Masses with his whole heart has got it right. For who does not himself know highs and lows, the cross and suffering? And certain death awaits us all. But then comes Easter. The tomb does not have the last word. Holy Week tells us this, because it is true for us as well.

The Passion in the Gospel of John 19:16–35

Then he handed him over to them to be crucified.

So they took Jesus, and he went out, bearing his own cross, to the place called the place of a skull, which is called in Hebrew Golgotha. There they crucified him, and with him two others, one on either side, and Jesus between them. Pilate also wrote a title and put it on the cross; it read, "Jesus of Nazareth, the King of the Jews." Many of the Jews read this title, for the place where Jesus was crucified was near the city; and it was written in Hebrew, in Latin, and in Greek. The chief priests of the Jews then said to Pilate, "Do not write, 'The King of the Jews,' but, 'This man said, I am King of the Jews.'" Pilate answered, "What I have written I have written."

When the soldiers had crucified Jesus they took his garments and made four parts, one for each soldier; also his tunic. But the tunic was without seam, woven from top to bottom; so they said to one another, "Let us not tear it, but cast lots for it to see whose it shall be." This was to fulfil the Scripture,

"They parted my garments among them,
and for my clothing they cast lots."

So the soldiers did this. But standing by the cross of Jesus were his mother, and his mother's sister, Mary the wife of Clopas, and Mary Magdalene. When Jesus saw his mother, and the disciple whom he loved standing near, he said to his mother, "Woman, behold, your son!" Then

*he said to the disciple, "Behold, your mother!" And from
that hour the disciple took her to his own home.*

*After this Jesus, knowing that all was now finished,
said (to fulfil the Scripture), "I thirst." A bowl full of
vinegar stood there; so they put a sponge full of the vinegar on hyssop and held it to his mouth. When Jesus had
received the vinegar, he said, "It is finished"; and he bowed
his head and gave up his spirit.*

*Since it was the day of Preparation, in order to prevent
the bodies from remaining on the cross on the sabbath (for
that sabbath was a high day), the Jews asked Pilate that
their legs might be broken, and that they might be taken
away. So the soldiers came and broke the legs of the first,
and of the other who had been crucified with him; but
when they came to Jesus and saw that he was already
dead, they did not break his legs. But one of the soldiers
pierced his side with a spear, and at once there came out
blood and water. He who saw it has borne witness—his
testimony is true, and he knows that he tells the truth—
that you also may believe.*

(Complete text: Jn 18:1–Jn 19:42)

❧

Thoughts on the Passion in the Gospel of John

Everything about this text is sober. Not a word about feelings. Simple description: he carried his Cross. They crucified him. A sign up on the Cross. They throw dice to see
who will get his coat. At the Cross, three women, among
them his own mother. Here, at last, we expect a word of

sympathy: his own mother! She had to watch it all! Her own son in these agonies! To have to stand by and watch helplessly: Can there be anything worse for a mother?

It is exactly this completely sober type of report that gives the words such power. The place of execution was close to the city. The drama was repeated frequently. The many passers-by were accustomed to watching the terrible death agonies of the crucified, as we are accustomed to the daily deaths on our streets: Another person is dying there again!

But this one man, who was crucified between two nameless men on the day before the Jewish Easter feast, is different. His name is not forgotten. Because the one who died there was God's Son. And his death was not an accident; rather, he voluntarily took this path, for us, not for himself.

Beneath the cool, calm words of the report, the fire of this "for us" burns. He looks after his mother and his favorite disciple, John, and with that entrusts everyone to the protection of his mother.

"I thirst": not just the agony of the death throes, but the thirst for our faith, that we will trust him in life and in death. He will never leave us.

He truly lives forever now for us.

EASTER

The Gospel of Matthew 28:1–10

Now after the sabbath, toward the dawn of the first day of the week, Mary Magdalene and the other Mary went to see the tomb. And behold, there was a great earthquake; for an angel of the Lord descended from heaven and came and rolled back the stone, and sat upon it. His appearance was like lightning, and his clothing white as snow. And for fear of him the guards trembled and became like dead men. But the angel said to the women, "Do not be afraid; for I know that you seek Jesus who was crucified. He is not here; for he has risen, as he said. Come, see the place where he lay. Then go quickly and tell his disciples that he has risen from the dead, and behold, he is going before you to Galilee; there you will see him. Behold, I have told you." So they departed quickly from the tomb with fear and great joy, and ran to tell his disciples. And behold, Jesus met them and said, "Hail!" And they came up and took hold of his feet and worshiped him. Then Jesus said to them, "Do not be afraid; go and tell my brethren to go to Galilee, and there they will see me."

෨෧

He Is Not Here

No one was a witness to what happened that night, probably shortly before daybreak. Jesus had died on Friday around three in the afternoon after agonizing hours hanging on the Cross. His apostles were conspicuous in their absence, except for John, who held out with Jesus' mother at the Cross. What was to be done with the body?

In their panic and utter dejection, the apostles had not thought about it at all. There were two respected men, though, who performed what is the simplest act of human decency: to provide for a burial. One of them, Joseph of Arimathea, had had a tomb carved for himself in the cliffs close by the "place of the skull", Golgotha; it could be sealed with a heavy stone that could be rolled. There they laid the body of Jesus in makeshift fashion.

Matthew reports, moreover, that the Jewish authorities had the tomb guarded by soldiers and sealed with the stone, "lest his disciples go and steal him away and tell the people: He has risen from the dead."

The next day was the Sabbath. Everyone had to rest according to Jewish custom. But two days later, very early on the morning of the first day of the new week, which we call Sunday, the women went to the tomb, much like mourners who are drawn to the grave of their loved ones still do today. What they experienced there is the start of a completely new story. They saw how the stone had been rolled away; a messenger of God, an angel, spoke to them: "He is not here, for he has risen." They looked inside: the tomb was empty. It must already have been empty when the stone was still sealed in front of it, guarded by soldiers. What had happened?

No one had been a witness to this event. But the outcome was obvious: "He is not here."

Carrying him away was beyond anyone's ability. The confusion was great, a mixture of fear and joy. Had he not said he would rise from the dead? But what does that mean?

Everything would have remained unclear if the other thing had not been added: that he showed himself, first to the women, then to the apostles and a whole host of others. They all declared firmly and clearly that they saw him, touched him, that he spoke with them. They all testify to this fact: He lives! But not as he had lived before, in a mortal body, but in a completely different way: He appeared, came through closed doors, and then was suddenly gone.

Were they having hallucinations? Mass delusions? If that had been the case, then the little band of his "fans" would have quickly dispersed again. The fact of the matter is that up to this day people throughout the world, even without having seen him, say: He lives!

We experience his presence, his nearness and help. We believe: He is risen! This is the joy of Easter.

The Gospel of John 20:19–31

On the evening of that day, the first day of the week, the doors being shut where the disciples were, for fear of the Jews, Jesus came and stood among them and said to them, "Peace be with you." When he had said this, he showed them his hands and his side. Then the disciples were glad when they saw the Lord. Jesus said to them again, "Peace be with you. As the Father has sent me, even so I send you." And when he had said this, he breathed on them, and said to them, "Receive the Holy Spirit. If you forgive the sins of any, they are forgiven; if you retain the sins of any, they are retained."

Now Thomas, one of the Twelve, called the Twin, was not with them when Jesus came. So the other disciples told him, "We have seen the Lord." But he said to them, "Unless I see in his hands the print of the nails, and place my finger in the mark of the nails, and place my hand in his side, I will not believe."

Eight days later, his disciples were again in the house, and Thomas was with them. The doors were shut, but Jesus came and stood among them, and said, "Peace be with you." Then he said to Thomas, "Put your finger here, and see my hands; and put out your hand, and place it in my side; do not be faithless, but believing." Thomas answered him, "My Lord and my God!" Jesus said to him, "You have believed because you have seen me. Blessed are those who have not seen and yet believe."

Now Jesus did many other signs in the presence of the disciples, which are not written in this book; but these are written that you may believe that Jesus is the Christ, the Son of God, and that believing you may have life in his name.

❧

Doubting Thomas

How can we not like him, the doubting Thomas, who is full of questions and does not dare ask them! Of course, it is not very easy to believe that the teacher with whom they were on the move for three years and who met such a horribly brutal end could be alive, that he could simply be there again, completely alive and in the flesh. That Thomas has doubts about this, who could hold that against him?

Now back to the scene of the crime. Jesus has been laid in a rock tomb near the place of execution, Golgotha. Two days later, in the morning, the women are at the tomb; they find it open, but they do not find him inside of it. Has someone taken the body away? Then Mary Magdalene sees a man whom she takes to be the gardener: "Did you take him away? Where have you laid him?" The man addresses her by name: "Mary!" Then she recognizes him: "Rabbi! Teacher!" She hurries to the apostles and tells them: "I have seen the Lord" (cf. Jn 20:11–18).

This is where today's Gospel begins. They do not give much credence to this woman, those eleven men, who have locked the doors tightly in fear. They hold her words to be idle chatter, as Luke very honestly reports (Lk 24:11). And the situation is dangerous. They have arrested and executed Jesus; why should they not be next?

What then happened is difficult to comprehend, but they testify unwaveringly that it was so: Suddenly Jesus is there, among them, despite the locked doors. That it is he, there is no doubt: he shows the nail holes in his hands and the large wound in his side from the lance thrust, which was given to make sure of his death—not bleeding wounds, not even ones healed over, but ... well, how can you imagine something that falls outside our realm of experience?

Thomas, who was not there, wants to see, touch, in the literal sense, "grasp". Otherwise, he simply cannot believe something so truly incredible.

A week later, on this very day, the time has come. Jesus is suddenly standing there among them again. Now Thomas can truly "grasp" that he lives. And now he believes. Now he can say with his whole heart: "My Lord and my God!"

But how are we to comprehend what is incomprehensible to us because it remains invisible? Not seeing and yet believing, this is how we should be, Jesus says to Thomas. But can one believe without reason, simply leap into the unknown? Jesus does not expect this. There are reasons to believe, reasons to trust: first, the credibility of those who actually saw Jesus at that time, especially the doubting Thomas—they did not have hallucinations; then the testimonial of the many generations thereafter and to this day, who indeed have not seen the Risen One but have, in faith, felt his closeness, his spirit, his love.

"Peace be with you" were his first words at that time. This peace is still there to this day, whenever in the midst of fear and need I suddenly experience a peace that does not originate from within me.

For I know: He is risen and is with us.

THIRD SUNDAY OF EASTER

The Gospel of John 21:1–14

After this Jesus revealed himself again to the disciples by the Sea of Tiberias; and he revealed himself in this way. Simon Peter, Thomas called the Twin, Nathanael of Cana in Galilee, the sons of Zebedee, and two others of his disciples were together. Simon Peter said to them, "I am going fishing." They said to him, "We will go with you." They went out and got into the boat; but that night they caught nothing.

Just as day was breaking, Jesus stood on the beach; yet the disciples did not know that it was Jesus. Jesus said to them, "Children, have you any fish?" They answered him, "No." He said to them, "Cast the net on the right side of the boat, and you will find some." So they cast it, and now they were not able to haul it in, for the quantity of fish. That disciple whom Jesus loved said to Peter, "It is the Lord!" When Simon Peter heard that it was the Lord, he put on his clothes, for he was stripped for work, and sprang into the sea. But the other disciples came in the boat, dragging the net full of fish, for they were not far from the land, but about a hundred yards off.

When they got out on land, they saw a charcoal fire there, with fish lying on it, and bread. Jesus said to them, "Bring some of the fish that you have just caught." So Simon Peter went aboard and hauled the net ashore, full of large fish, a hundred and fifty-three of them; and although there were so many, the net was not torn. Jesus said to them, "Come and have breakfast." Now none of the disciples dared ask him, "Who are you?" They knew it was the Lord. Jesus came and took the bread and gave it to them, and so with the fish. This was now the third time that Jesus was revealed to the disciples after he was raised from the dead.

୨ଈ

Life Goes On

They are again in their homeland, having returned to Galilee to their old occupation as fishermen. After all, they have to live on something. At that time, three years earlier, when it all began, when Jesus of Nazareth called them to come with him, they left everything, their boats, their families; they relied completely on him, did not care for tomorrow, because they trusted that he would even take care of that. And even when they were poor and at times hardly had the bare minimum to eat, they nevertheless experienced that, in their wandering life with Jesus, God provided for them, good people supported them. And above all there was the great hope: their Master, on whom they had staked everything, would soon establish the "kingdom of God" in Israel, and then everything would be different; there would be an end to need and poverty, and they, as they thought in secret, would then receive good positions in his kingdom.

And then it all happened quite differently: he was increasingly rejected, persecuted, condemned, and finally hung on the Cross. With his death, it was all over. Three days after the catastrophe, in fact, there came a further change: they found his tomb empty, and he even appeared to them, several times. Now they knew that he was alive. But not in the same way as before, no longer here, but "over there", no longer as their beloved Master with whom you could move from place to place, visible and tangible.

Now they have to pick up their own lives again. He is already living again on the other side, beyond death; they have to toil away further in this life. So they return to their old occupation: they go fishing. And like so often, it is arduous: not a fish in the net the whole night long!

As the day is breaking there on the sea, someone is standing on the shore and calling out to them. At his word, they go ahead and throw the net out one more time, and now it is full to the point of tearing.

It is the Lord! John, his favorite disciple, is the first to recognize him. He is there, not like before, but he is truly there; he talks with them; they eat with him.

And this is the experience of his followers to this day. Life goes on: work, daily life, difficulties, and joys. But he awaits us on the shore of eternal life. He is already over there, while we are still on the way there in the vessel of our life. He actually announced it himself: I go to prepare you a dwelling place. We hope some day to be received there, to be pulled onto the good shore in the great fishing net of Saint Peter, to be among the 153 large fish. Whoever has this hope has a different orientation in life.

Yes, life goes on, even after Easter. But it has become different, because it has a goal, a direction, because it has become a journey home, where he awaits us.

FOURTH SUNDAY OF EASTER

The Gospel of John 10:1–10

"Truly, truly, I say to you, he who does not enter the sheepfold by the door but climbs in by another way, that man is a thief and a robber; but he who enters by the door is the shepherd of the sheep. To him the gatekeeper opens; the sheep hear his voice, and he calls his own sheep by name and leads them out. When he has brought out all his own, he goes before them, and the sheep follow him, for they know his voice. A stranger they will not follow, but they will flee from him, for they do not know the voice of strangers." This figure Jesus used with them, but they did not understand what he was saying to them.

So Jesus again said to them, "Truly, truly, I say to you, I am the door of the sheep. All who came before me are thieves and robbers; but the sheep did not heed them. I am the door; if any one enters by me, he will be saved, and will go in and out and find pasture. The thief comes only to steal and kill and destroy; I came that they may have life, and have it abundantly."

The Door to Life

The fourth Sunday in the Easter season is called Good Shepherd Sunday.

185

Jesus called himself the Good Shepherd. Christian art has been fond of portraying him as such.

It is a beautiful, soothing image: the shepherd, who worries about his herd, protects it from thieves and wild animals, who brings the lost sheep home on his shoulders out of danger.

In today's passage, however, Jesus uses a different word picture. He calls himself the door to the sheep. And he makes clear: He who does not enter the sheepfold by the door is a thief and a robber who does not want to protect, but rather wants to steal. He forces his entry with evil intent.

This parable from the rural life familiar to everyone at that time comes to an admittedly frightening head when Jesus then clarifies: All who came before me are thieves and robbers!

Is this not terribly presumptuous and intolerant, that Jesus simply writes off all those who do not follow him? Can this be accepted without protest? That is why it is not surprising that it says at the end of the passage: "There was again a division among the Jews because of these words. Many of them said, 'He has a demon, and he is mad; why listen to him?' Others said, 'These are not the sayings of one who has a demon. Can a demon open the eyes of the blind?'" (Jn 10:19–21).

Was Jesus intolerant? Was he what would today be called a fundamentalist or even a religious fanatic who grossly overestimated himself and despised others? This is how his enemies saw him, and that is why they persecuted and eventually killed him.

Or is the parable of the shepherd and the door something like a mirror in which it is unpleasant to look, especially for those of us who are called to be shepherds and are supposed to be shepherds (bishops, priests, but also everyone who bears responsibility for others)? The question Jesus poses to us is very simple: Are you interested in others or only in yourselves? Do you want only to fulfill yourselves, or are you concerned first and foremost with the well-being of those entrusted to you?

And so that it is clear how serious the choice is, he says: Anyone who only looks out for himself is a thief and a robber. Anyone who pursues only his own wishes in his own children robs them and prevents them from being able to develop themselves. Anyone who seeks only his own self-fulfillment in his spouse steals that person's own room for growth and life. Any priest who thinks only about his popularity is no shepherd; rather, he is a thief of the hearts of men. He deceives them of their trust.

People have found Jesus to be different from all this. He came, not to garner attention, but to give life. This is why his word was so different from the empty talk we engage in. His voice had an unmistakable tone. "He calls his own sheep by name and leads them out." It is the voice of God, which sometimes penetrates the din of our daily life into our hearts. And then it becomes clear: Only when we go through these doors are we saved.

Jesus alone is this door that God has opened to us so that we will not go astray.

Fifth Sunday of Easter

The Gospel of John 14:1–12

"Let not your hearts be troubled; believe in God, believe also in me. In my Father's house are many rooms; if it were not so, would I have told you that I go to prepare a place for you? And when I go and prepare a place for you, I will come again and will take you to myself, that where I am you may be also. And you know the way where I am going." Thomas said to him, "Lord, we do not know where you are going; how can we know the way?" Jesus said to him, "I am the way, and the truth, and the life; no one comes to the Father, but by me. If you had known me, you would have known my Father also; henceforth you know him and have seen him."

Philip said to him, "Lord, show us the Father, and we shall be satisfied." Jesus said to him, "Have I been with you so long, and yet you do not know me, Philip? He who has seen me has seen the Father; how can you say, 'Show us the Father'? Do you not believe that I am in the Father and the Father is in me? The words that I say to you I do not speak on my own authority; but the Father who dwells in me does his works. Believe me that I am in the Father and the Father in me; or else believe me for the sake of the works themselves.

"Truly, truly, I say to you, he who believes in me will also do the works that I do; and greater works than these will he do, because I go to the Father."

The Journey Is the Goal

We are on the way as long as we are in this world. Our life is a journey.

We talk about our "journey through life" when we look back at what lies behind us. For the most part, it has not been a perfectly straight road; often it has not even been clearly delineated; nor has it been a broad, even, comfortable road. There have even been detours from time to time, steep and stony stretches of road, and then meandering and wrong ways, but it has always been and continues to be an "on the way". Not until life's end is the journey of life over. And then at last the question arises of whether it has led to the goal.

Jesus is talking about this goal in today's Gospel, which belongs to the words that he spoke on the last evening before his violent death. They are words of parting. But instead of the apostles comforting him, for whom such terrible things are in store, he comforts them. He speaks of a reunion over there "in my father's house". He promises all those who are now confused and sad that he will not leave them all alone: I go before you; I will prepare a place for you there, and then I will come get you so that we are always together, there, where there is no more death and there are no tears.

We sense here what a great heart Jesus has: not a word about his own, imminent suffering, just loving care of his friends. He comforts them: For each of you there is a place prepared there. But what good is this absolutely beautiful prospect of the eternal home if we do not know the way there?

Show us the way there, says the doubting Thomas, who always wants to know everything exactly. In reply, Jesus points to himself: "I am the way!" No one comes home, to the eternal goal, "but by me".

Is this not presumptuous? How can a man call himself the way, indeed, the only way leading to the goal? Similarly, on the previous Sunday Jesus called himself the only door through which one can enter into eternal life. Is he, then, the "only one able to save"? Moreover, he calls himself not only the way, but the goal as well, which is even farther-reaching: "I am the way, the truth and the life."

It is quite understandable why people at that time, like people today, thought he was a blasphemer or was simply crazy. And it is not surprising that they thought the same thing about his followers.

I consider there to be only one answer: Each man must seek his own way through life. For two thousand years, many have found Jesus to be the only way, and they have borne witness that they have traveled well on this way.

They have trusted him, staked all on him, and he has not disappointed them: they have truly found life.

The Gospel of John 14:15–21

"If you love me, you will keep my commandments. And I will ask the Father, and he will give you another Counselor, to be with you for ever, even the Spirit of truth, whom the world cannot receive, because it neither sees him nor knows him; you know him, for he dwells with you, and will be in you.

"I will not leave you desolate; I will come to you. Yet a little while, and the world will see me no more, but you will see me; because I live, you will live also. In that day you will know that I am in my Father, and you in me, and I in you. He who has my commandments and keeps them, he it is who loves me; and he who loves me will be loved by my Father, and I will love him and manifest myself to him."

୫

The Other Comforter

Pentecost is drawing nearer, not just an extended, busy weekend, a time for relaxation for many, but the feast of the Holy Spirit. Jesus announces the Holy Spirit's coming; he promises that he will send another Counselor and calls him the "Spirit of truth". But who is he, this invisible, unknown one? Who is the Holy Spirit?

I can picture Jesus. I see him in my mind's eye as he goes in Galilee from village to village, as people crowd around him, as he gets into a boat or walks alone to the mountain to pray. I can grasp all of that; I have seen the land where he lived, the shore of the lake of Gennesaret, Jerusalem, where he was killed and where the empty tomb can be seen.

But the Holy Spirit—how am I supposed to picture him? Jesus promised not that we would be able to see him, but that he would be definitely recognizable by his effects. Jesus discusses two of these today in the Gospel.

First, he calls him "another Counselor". The biblical word *paraclete* can be translated in various ways: helper, intercessor, advocate, comforter, counselor. Jesus was all of these things to his friends. He is no longer visibly here now. But he promised that he would not leave us all alone, because another Comforter would stay with us. How do I recognize that he is there?

I become aware of the Holy Spirit, for example, when comfort suddenly enters my heart in times of difficulty, even more so when I feel the strength to give comfort and support to others, although I am suffering myself. It is certainly the Holy Spirit who gives such comfort.

But the surest sign that he is at work is, without a doubt, love. The Spirit of Jesus is certainly there wherever love is found, especially wherever it overcomes enmity, builds bridges, summons up patience, heals wounds.

Time and again, I meet people who have developed an excellent feel for this activity of the Holy Spirit. They experience him like an inner compass, I would almost say, as a friend, who comforts, advises, supports, who is simply always there.

Jesus also calls him the "Spirit of truth". "What is truth?" (Jn 18:38), Pilate asked Jesus. Who knows already what truth is? But Jesus says very definitely: The Holy Spirit will guide you into all truth. It helps again to see what the biblical word for truth means. It means steadfastness, reliability, loyalty. For the Bible, a true man is one who is honest, reliable, not fickle, and not moody. Jesus promises this Spirit of rectitude and steadfastness. Whoever lets himself be led by the One who can be relied on will himself become for others a comfort and support, a genuine helper and friend.

The apostles turned into such men, they who had previously run away out of fear. Jesus promised them this "power from above", and one can see in their lives that they in fact became brave, upright men, ready for action. How very much we need such "Spirit-filled" people today! Why should we not become such people ourselves?

ASCENSION OF CHRIST

The Gospel of Matthew 28:16–20

Now the eleven disciples went to Galilee, to the mountain to which Jesus had directed them. And when they saw him they worshiped him; but some doubted. And Jesus came and said to them, "All authority in heaven and on earth has been given to me. Go therefore and make disciples of all nations, baptizing them in the name of the Father and of the Son and of the Holy Spirit, teaching them to observe all that I have commanded you; and behold, I am with you always, to the close of the age."

❧

Jesus Kept His Word

These are the last verses of the Gospel of Matthew, which are read at Mass on the Feast of the Ascension of Christ. They have an enormous range of implications; their repercussions have made world history. It is the global, borderless commission of Jesus: They are to go to all nations, make all men disciples of Jesus, baptizing them and teaching them everything Jesus said. And along with that, the incomprehensible message that Jesus has been given (by God) all authority, in heaven and on earth, that is, everywhere! It cannot be any clearer; it cannot be any more comprehensive.

The scene takes place where everything began: in Galilee, the region that was home to Jesus and his first disciples, on a mountain, just as Jesus initially explained his "program", the "Sermon on the Mount", on a mountain overlooking the Sea of Gennesaret.

At that time there were twelve apostles; now one is missing: Judas, who betrayed Jesus and then killed himself in despair. In the meantime there has been the catastrophe of Jerusalem, when they sentenced him to death on the Cross in a dubious trial and executed him. They all ran away, in fear and panic, helpless.

But then the incredible Easter morning came: the tomb empty and a message to return to Galilee, where they would see him. When they then in fact saw him, a few doubted, all too understandably, because everything they had experienced was too much to handle.

And yet, despite the questions and doubts, they completely committed themselves to the task: they set out from their home in Galilee and reached "the ends of the earth", bringing the message of Jesus to all nations. And today there is in fact hardly a corner of the globe that the gospel has not yet reached.

There is also doubt today. Was it actually good, helpful, to spread this message everywhere? And were the messengers truly always bringers of the good news of Jesus? Did they not often serve worldly power interests as well? How was it then here? In Roman times, when soldiers (like Saint Florian) or monks (like Saint Severin) first lived in our land and then taught the gospel? How was it with the Irish monks who evangelized our lands anew back then? How was it when, in the nineteenth century, thousands upon thousands of people from our lands became missionaries on other continents? And how is it today when people from Asia,

Africa, and America remind us in old Europe again of the original good news?

They all received the commission of Jesus and translated it into action, and that is how the gospel truly went to the ends of the earth.

In Nigeria, for example, I myself have seen how the work of missionaries from Ireland (as happened a thousand years ago here) have produced magnificent fruits. They planted a blossoming young Church there, which today is standing on her own legs and is herself sending out missionaries to all nations in Africa.

When discussing the missionary history of Christianity, it is a great injustice to emphasize only the negative aspects, which there were as well. It is magnificent how, through thousands of years, Jesus' directive to offer all people the chance to become his disciples has been tirelessly translated into action. But it is even more magnificent that Jesus kept his own promise: "And behold, I am with you always, to the close of the age." Without this pledge, the Christian mission would never have been successful. What I experienced in Nigeria has always been the secret of the mission: people do not just accept a teaching superficially; they become believers to the core, who can experience in their lives and therefore attest to the fact: Christ is truly with us, with us always. Jesus has truly kept his word.

The Gospel of John 17:1–11a

When Jesus had spoken these words, he lifted up his eyes to heaven and said, "Father, the hour has come; glorify your Son that the Son may glorify you, since you have given him power over all flesh, to give eternal life to all whom you have given him. And this is eternal life, that they know you the only true God, and Jesus Christ whom you have sent. I glorified you on earth, having accomplished the work which you gave me to do; and now, Father, glorify you me in your own presence with the glory which I had with you before the world was made.

"I have manifested your name to the men whom you gave me out of the world; yours they were, and you gave them to me, and they have kept your word. Now they know that everything that you have given me is from you; for I have given them the words which you gave me, and they have received them and know in truth that I came from you; and they have believed that you did send me. I am praying for them; I am not praying for the world but for those whom you have given me, for they are yours; all mine are yours, and yours are mine, and I am glorified in them. And now I am no more in the world, but they are in the world, and I am coming to you. Holy Father, keep them in your name, which you have given me, that they may be one, even as we are one."

197

To the Glory of God

Not everything belongs in the public eye. There is a sphere of intimacy that should be protected. Personal prayer belongs to this sphere as well. What I bring before God in my innermost heart is my secret, which only God and I know about. It is a little embarrassing when someone exposes his most personal affairs. In certain moments, it is, of course, different. We see such a moment in today's Gospel.

It is the night before his death. Jesus is together with his disciples. In this serious hour, he speaks words of parting. He entrusts his friends with what moves him; he opens his heart to them. After he has spoken to them at length (in the Gospel of John, chapters 13–15) he gets even more personal: he prays in front of them. It is the only longer personal prayer of Jesus that has come down to us. It is often reported that he withdrew to the solitude of the mountains to be alone with God. The Gospels, with few exceptions, are silent about the content of his prayers.

The first word of his prayer in this long night is: Father!

In Jesus' circle, it must have had a very particular sound to it. In the early Church, they remembered that he used the childlike "Abba" for this, "Papa" or "Daddy". We should also address God with this word when we pray the Our Father.

There is an attitude behind this word: one of trust, complete confidence, not fear and terror, but closeness and faith.

"Father, the hour has come!" This solemn word points to what is in store, the hour of suffering, the approaching hour of death, the end. The final hour has struck. Jesus knows how it will look. But there is no panic, no despair in this word. It is not the fear of a hopeless man. It almost sounds certain of victory: The decisive hour has come, and it will not mean the end.

Jesus asks God: Glorify me that I may glorify you.

Strange words in the face of death! But they let us sense something about what is really moving Jesus in his heart, what it was really all about for him. Whether his friends understood him? Whether we really understand? Jesus has a single great concern: that God be glorified! In the language of the Bible, the phrase is often found: "Glory to God in the highest." What does that mean: to glorify God?

The people of the Middle Ages knew: they built Saint Stephen's Cathedral "to the glory of God". Mozart, Haydn, Schubert composed many works to proclaim the glory of God. Who is not familiar with the thought of God's grandeur and majesty when they experience a magnificent day in the mountains?

Jesus has this as his first and greatest concern: that the God he calls Father be glorified. He wants God to be recognized and acknowledged. For this he risks his life, to the utmost. Counterquestion: Does God need our praise, then? Certainly not. But this is also certain: Where God is great, man is not small. Where God is honored, man is held in high regard.

And that is exactly why it says: "Glory to God in the highest—and on earth peace among men!"

The Gospel of John 20:19–23

On the evening of that day, the first day of the week, the doors being shut where the disciples were, for fear of the Jews, Jesus came and stood among them and said to them, "Peace be with you." When he had said this, he showed them his hands and his side. Then the disciples were glad when they saw the Lord. Jesus said to them again, "Peace be with you. As the Father has sent me, even so I send you." And when he had said this, he breathed on them, and said to them, "Receive the Holy Spirit. If you forgive the sins of any, they are forgiven; if you retain the sins of any, they are retained."

❧

Reason Enough to Celebrate!

Again an extended, busy weekend. Schoolchildren look forward to the short vacation; the business world groans over the many holidays in May. Why we actually have them, what their origins are, whom we have to thank for them—we should definitely think about these things much more. I sincerely invite everyone to do so.

Today is Pentecost. Like so many Christian feasts, this one also has a Jewish origin. It was called the "Feast of

Weeks"—in Judaism, the feast of Pesach—it was and is celebrated seven weeks, fifty days, after Easter.

Originally it arose as a thanksgiving celebration at the end of the grain harvest, which took place in the Holy Land much earlier than in our country. But in the Jewish cycle of festivals, God's revelation and the giving of the national covenant on Mount Sinai are also remembered at Pentecost.

The Christian meaning of the Feast of Pentecost is also derived from Easter. Jesus Christ did not remain in the grave; he rose from the dead and is living. He continues to work; he "in-spires" his disciples, that is, he gives them of his Spirit so that they can carry on his work everywhere, in all languages, to all peoples.

This happened on Pentecost when the small group of the original Church—around 120 people—were together in Jerusalem and received the "power from above" that Jesus had promised. From that point on, there began the great adventure of spreading the gospel, which truly reached all nations, in hundreds of languages. It is an inspiring thing to experience this universality of Jesus' message, for instance, on the great feast days in Rome. In my travels, I always experience anew how people from the most divergent cultures, languages, and nations live by the power of the Christian faith. This makes the Spirit of Pentecost concrete.

The Gospel that is read today, of course, leads back again to what happened fifty days earlier, to the eve of Easter. At that point, there was no evidence yet of spreading worldwide. A small, frightened band, eleven apostles (Judas is no longer there), behind tightly shut doors. They are afraid. Jesus has been killed, so now it can happen to them as well.

Then suddenly Jesus stands in their midst, unhindered by locks and walls. And into their fear he speaks his "Peace be with you!" And when they see his nail wounds from the Cross, every doubt is dispersed: It is he; he lives! And they should live! They should cast off their fear, let themselves be sent out by him to all men, just as God the Father sent him to us men. For this they need his staying power, and that is why he breathes on them, so that his Spirit may be in them. And that can only mean: Just as he came to bring God's mercy, so are they to forgive sins in his name, remove the burdens of guilt, for that is the good news of Jesus. And they themselves will also need to be forgiven time and again, because they will also have faults, will commit sins, will have to ask for forgiveness.

Easter and Pentecost are not just extended weekends; they are feasts of a happy message, which really is reason enough for celebrating. Happy Pentecost!

FEASTS IN THE CHURCH YEAR

The Gospel of John 3:16–18

*For God so loved the world that he gave his only-
begotten Son, that whoever believes in him should not
perish but have eternal life. For God sent the Son into
the world, not to condemn the world, but that the world
might be saved through him. He who believes in him is
not condemned; he who does not believe is condemned
already, because he has not believed in the name of the
only-begotten Son of God.*

ॐ

Save, Do Not Condemn!

There are words that Jesus spoke in the Gospel that never
let go of you again once they have found their way into
your own heart. Today's words are such words: "For God
so loved the world that . . ." and "not to condemn, but to
save".

But in order for these very comforting and benevolent
words of Jesus to strike root in our hearts, it is helpful to
look at them more closely. For Jesus says them in a very
specific context. He speaks these words in a long nighttime
discussion with a Jewish councilor named Nicodemus, who
initially came only in secret to Jesus to ask him his questions, out of fear of his colleagues. Later, however, he has

the courage to stand up publicly for Jesus and, finally, together with Joseph of Arimathea, even to take Jesus down from the Cross and to give him a dignified burial.

This Nicodemus probably senses that Jesus has come from God and can show the way to life. But what Jesus says to him is rather enigmatic, not only for those times, but still today.

Shortly before our Gospel text, Jesus says to Nicodemus that he must "be lifted up" like Moses "lifted up" the serpent in the wilderness. Nicodemus understands the allusion. When the people of Israel were in the wilderness near Sinai, they had to endure poisonous snakes. Then Moses set a metal snake on a pole and everyone who looked at the snake was healed of the poisonous snakebites (Num 21:4–9).

Thus, Jesus is indicating to Nicodemus that he will be hung on the Cross, so that anyone who trustingly looks up to the Cross will find healing. It must have been difficult for this Jewish councilor to understand these words. He had expected something quite different in his hope that Jesus would be the Messiah, the liberator, that Jesus would bring justice, freedom, and order, that he would condemn the opponents of Israel and destroy the enemies of God, so that peace might finally come upon this world full of blood and tears.

Instead, Jesus tells him: God loved the world so much that he gave his Son for us. Jesus tells him: The peace you long for, God gives to you through me. Look up to the Cross; then you will see how much God loves you. Look up at me; believe me; trust me; I have come, not to condemn men, but to save them.

Jesus often showed how he meant this; for instance, when they dragged the adulteress before him to stone her to death, and he said to the accusers: "Let him who is without sin among you be the first to throw a stone." When they had gone, he said to her: "Neither do I condemn you; go, and do not sin again" (Jn 8:7–11).

Thus, I want to believe firmly with Nicodemus: You, Lord, do not condemn and do not despise me, even when others condemn me and I condemn myself. You came, not to reproach me with a criminal record, but to free me of it. At the same time, however, you expect me to believe and trust you and, myself, to give to others what you give to me: Do not condemn, but save!

Corpus Christi

The Gospel of John 6:51–58

"I am the living bread which came down from heaven; if any one eats of this bread, he will live for ever; and the bread which I shall give for the life of the world is my flesh."

The Jews then disputed among themselves, saying, "How can this man give us his flesh to eat?" So Jesus said to them, "Truly, truly, I say to you, unless you eat the flesh of the Son of man and drink his blood, you have no life in you; he who eats my flesh and drinks my blood has eternal life, and I will raise him up at the last day. For my flesh is food indeed, and my blood is drink indeed. He who eats my flesh and drinks my blood abides in me, and I in him. As the living Father sent me, and I live because of the Father, so he who eats me will live because of me. This is the bread which came down from heaven, not such as the fathers ate and died; he who eats this bread will live for ever."

❧

Jesus—Life-Giving Food!

Jesus does not make it simple for his listeners at that time in Capernaum, the little village on the Sea of Gennesaret, where he says in the synagogue (the ruins of which still stand today) those enigmatic words to his countrymen: "He who eats my flesh and drinks my blood abides in me, and I in him."

They take offense at this, as one can well understand. They ask: How can he give us his flesh to eat? But Jesus sticks with it, says it explicitly, provokingly, and clearly: "He who eats my flesh and drinks my blood has eternal life!"

That is too much, even for many of his closest followers: What he is saying is unbearable! Who can listen to this? And John the Evangelist, who was there himself, reports that many disciples turn away from Jesus and leave him at that time.

Do they misunderstand Jesus? Does he not mean that metaphorically, symbolically? He cannot possibly mean that we really should eat his flesh and drink his blood. That would of course be a type of cannibalism. But why does Jesus not correct this? Why does he not hold them back when they begin to walk away, explain to them that it was a misunderstanding and that he did not mean it so literally? He does nothing of the sort. On the contrary, he intensifies his statement: "My flesh is food indeed, and my blood is drink indeed."

How does Jesus want these words to be understood? He offers some help himself: He calls himself the bread from heaven, which gives life. May I understand that in this way: Anyone who is connected with him finds life, just as bread keeps us alive? To be joined to God is vital to life, just as bread is: "He who eats this bread will live for ever", Jesus says.

But then again, is this not just meant symbolically, metaphorically? Jesus is obviously not merely describing a spiritual connection with God. We are to eat his flesh, and this really does mean a bodily contact, a real food. We mean exactly that when we believe that the little piece of bread, the Host, that we receive at Communion is the Body of Christ.

I will never forget this: A child—five years old—receives the Host by mistake from the priest and eats it, although it was not yet his First Holy Communion. Very excited, he hurries to his mother and says to her: "Mom, I have eaten God!" Childlike simplicity? Or childlike expression of a profound truth? It says the same thing that Jesus is saying: God gives himself as food so that we can live from him. Jesus—in the literal sense of our "life-giving food"—that is what we celebrate on the Feast of Corpus Christi. That deserves a holiday!

Immaculate Conception of Mary

The Gospel of Luke 1:26–38

*In the sixth month the angel Gabriel was sent from God
to a city of Galilee named Nazareth, to a virgin betrothed
to a man whose name was Joseph, of the house of David;
and the virgin's name was Mary. And he came to her and
said, "Hail, full of grace, the Lord is with you!" But she
was greatly troubled at the saying, and considered in her
mind what sort of greeting this might be. And the angel
said to her, "Do not be afraid, Mary, for you have found
favor with God. And behold, you will conceive in your
womb and bear a son, and you shall call his name Jesus.*

 *He will be great, and will be called the Son of the
  Most High;*
 *and the Lord God will give to him the throne of his
  father David,*
 and he will reign over the house of Jacob for ever;
 and of his kingdom there will be no end."

*And Mary said to the angel, "How can this be, since I
have no husband?" And the angel said to her,*

 "The Holy Spirit will come upon you,
 and the power of the Most High will overshadow you;
 therefore the child to be born will be called holy,
 the Son of God.

*And behold, your kinswoman Elizabeth in her old age has
also conceived a son; and this is the sixth month with her
who was called barren. For with God nothing will be impossible." And Mary said, "Behold, I am the handmaid of*

the Lord; let it be to me according to your word." And the
angel departed from her.

৶

Mary, the Favored One

December 8 is an especially important day for Austria. It
has played a role in the history of our country time and
again; people of faith have especially loved December 8.
Today we are in danger of no longer knowing at all what it
is about: One often says "Immaculate Conception" and thinks
this means the conception of Jesus, whom Mary conceived
by the Holy Spirit. Actually, it is about Mary's conception
by her parents, Joachim and Anna.

The Gospel for today is of course the Annunciation to
Mary. We celebrate the conception of Jesus in Mary's womb
through the work of the Holy Spirit on March 25—so why
do we hear precisely this Gospel today? Not because the
topic of today's feast is the conception of Jesus, but because
it is about the one whom the angel greets with the words:
"Hail Mary, full of grace!" These words are actually the
core of today's feast. What do they mean? Mary was wrapped
from the first moment of her conception, so to speak, in
the mantle of grace. She was preserved from the inheritance of every person who is born: original sin.

What is original sin? In Latin, it is perhaps clearer: *mac-
ula originalis*, it is called, the original stain we are born with,
but not in the sense of a spot, a contamination. Every person conceived is lacking something. He does not bring a
certain dimension with him to the world. And because he
lacks this dimension, as it were, from birth, he has a burden

that must be borne his whole life long. What is man lacking? The faith says that our progenitors lost God's friendship through their sins, through their turning away from God. Every person, so to speak, enters the world in a state of deficiency.

And now the Church announces and celebrates this mystery: Mary was born, as it were, without this deficiency. She is the only creature, the only human being, whom God gave in advance all that we, with difficulty in the course of our life, can and may obtain: friendship with God. She is completely blessed from the first moment on.

Can this be understood? Can a person be so blessed that, from the first moment on, no shadow exists between him and God? This is the mystery of Mary, and this is what we celebrate today. And why is this, of all feasts, so important for Austria? People in our country have felt: Mary is the person in whom there is no shadow of egotism, no shadow of selfishness, no shadow of sin. You can take refuge in her. That is why she has such a broad mantle; that is why all men have a place under this mantle, because she is completely "transparent" to the love of God, which enveloped her from the beginning. She is shrouded by the mantle of grace, and therefore every man can find room and refuge under her mantle, even though he might still be so pathetic and sin-laden. And that is why this feast is so wonderful, the fact that there is such a person who gave us Christ and who wants to be and is Mother to us all.

The Gospel of Luke 1:39–56

In those days Mary arose and went with haste into the hill country, to a city of Judah, and she entered the house of Zechariah and greeted Elizabeth. And when Elizabeth heard the greeting of Mary, the child leaped in her womb; and Elizabeth was filled with the Holy Spirit and she exclaimed with a loud cry, "Blessed are you among women, and blessed is the fruit of your womb! And why is this granted me, that the mother of my Lord should come to me? For behold, when the voice of your greeting came to my ears, the child in my womb leaped for joy. And blessed is she who believed that there would be a fulfilment of what was spoken to her from the Lord." And Mary said,

"My soul magnifies the Lord,
and my spirit rejoices in God my Savior,
for he has regarded the low estate of his handmaiden.
For behold, henceforth all generations will call me blessed;
for he who is mighty has done great things for me,
and holy is his name.
And his mercy is on those who fear him
from generation to generation.
He has shown strength with his arm,
he has scattered the proud in the imagination of their hearts,
he has put down the mighty from their thrones,
and exalted those of low degree;
he has filled the hungry with good things,
and the rich he has sent empty away.
He has helped his servant Israel,

in remembrance of his mercy,
as he spoke to our fathers,
to Abraham and to his posterity for ever."
And Mary remained with her about three months, and
returned to her home.

❧

A Celebration against Gravity

The universe is finite. It has a temporal beginning. It will
also have an end some day. Approximately fourteen billion
years ago, as scientists assume, it began with the Big Bang.
There was no "before that". And in billions of years, it will
finally fade away. Without an "after that"? Then was it all—
measured against eternity—only a brief enchantment?

We, too, are mortal. At one point we began to exist,
when the egg cell merged with a semen cell and started a
unique, never-before-existing and non-repeatable new creature: the moment when God called me into existence. Was
there no "me" before that? Not as that "I" who began to
exist at the moment of my conception.

But as the one who had already been "thought out" in God's
heart, in his thoughts, I existed in God's eternity. Even before
I was conceived in my mother's womb, God wanted and loved
me. I am not simply a "lucky shot" of nature; I am one of
God's thoughts, even if I have not by a long way translated
into reality what God intended me to be.

It is certain that my life will have an end, that I must die
some day. What will be after that? Simply "nothing"? Fad-
ing without a trace? Just as the entire universe will some
day burn out?

The Bible has a different message; it knows that death does not have the last word. The feast of the bodily reception of Mary into heaven (called the Assumption of Mary) could be called the "victory over entropy". Scientists understand entropy to be the inexorable movement toward extinction and death.

On the last page of the Bible there is this magnificent promise: "Then I saw a new heaven and a new earth.... And he who sat upon the throne said, Behold, I make all things new" (Rev 21:1, 5).

Even though everything we see today passes—our earth and all the stars and galaxies, and we ourselves—nevertheless, not everything will be devoured by death.

Why do we so particularly love and honor Mary? Because she is the beginning of this victory, "the dawning of the new creation". December 8—unfortunately in the meantime it has fallen prey to Christmas shopping—and August 15 are closely connected to each other. On December 8, we celebrate the conception of Mary in the womb of her mother, Anna. "Conceived without original sin", so the Church teaches about Mary, which means: without the seed of death, which we all carry in us. On August 15, we celebrate Mary's going home. "Blessed [*gebenedeit*] are you among women" is how Elizabeth greets her relative Mary, both of them pregnant. Mary is "great with child", as was said of pregnancy in the past. She was carrying Jesus at that time beneath her heart, the one who was to conquer our death through his.

The many portrayals of the Assumption of Mary usually show the apostles around an empty tomb. Death could not keep hold of this body that gave birth to Christ, our life, for us.

That is why Mary is the "hope of the new creation" and August 15 is such a joyful feast.

ALL SAINTS

The Gospel of Matthew 5:1–12a

Seeing the crowds, he went up on the mountain, and when he sat down his disciples came to him. And he opened his mouth and taught them, saying:

"Blessed are the poor in spirit, for theirs is the kingdom of heaven.

"Blessed are those who mourn, for they shall be comforted.

"Blessed are the meek, for they shall inherit the earth.

"Blessed are those who hunger and thirst for righteousness, for they shall be satisfied.

"Blessed are the merciful, for they shall obtain mercy.

"Blessed are the pure in heart, for they shall see God.

"Blessed are the peacemakers, for they shall be called sons of God.

"Blessed are those who are persecuted for righteousness' sake, for theirs is the kingdom of heaven.

"Blessed are you when men revile you and persecute you and utter all kinds of evil against you falsely on my account. Rejoice and be glad, for your reward is great in heaven."

৯৯

The Stuff Saints Are Made Of

On All Saints' Day the passage of the Gospel is read that, as I would like to say, presents the very heart of Jesus' message: the eight "Beatitudes". Their meaning is already visible when we consider the place and manner of their announcement.

We are on the seashore, on that hill that is still today called the "Mount of the Beatitudes". It is a uniquely beautiful sight that presents itself: before us the entire Sea of Gennesaret, on the left, the Golan Heights, on the right, the Valley of the Doves opens up, through which you can go up to Nazareth. A large crowd of people has gathered. Jesus begins to speak to them, more particularly to his disciples, who are to carry forth the teaching of their Master into the entire world one day.

The whole scene reminds us of another scene that was foundational for the Jewish people: at that time, on a different mountain, Mount Sinai, God communicated the Ten Commandments through Moses to the people in order to show all men the way to a happy life, individually and in society. Now God gives through his Son Jesus Christ yet another signpost to show the way, no longer in the form of prohibitions, but in the form of promises. Blessed is he who takes the paths shown here. He does not abolish the Ten Commandments; rather, he intensifies them.

"You shall not kill", the Fifth Commandment says. "Blessed are those who make no use of violence"; Jesus clarifies, "Blessed are the peacemakers." It is not enough "not to kill"; it is a matter of the innermost attitude of the heart. "Blessed are the merciful, for they shall obtain mercy."

The Seventh Commandment forbids theft. Every man knows in his heart that it is not right to steal another man's property. Our conscience tells us this, if we have not completely deadened it. But Jesus goes farther. He calls them blessed who "hunger and thirst for righteousness", that is, whose hearts burn when they see injustice, who do not look away when justice is violated. "Not stealing" is good; but it is better still to devote all one's energies toward creating more justice among us men.

The Sixth Commandment forbids adultery; and the Ninth and Tenth direct themselves against "covetousness", whether the neighbor's wife or his property. Jesus, however, is "radical"; he goes to the roots from which all wrong desire comes. "Blessed are the pure in heart, for they shall see God."

Happy, blessed is he who has become "upright" from the roots, whose heart has become whole and good. The first and the ninth Beatitudes show how our hearts can be "restored". To be poor before God makes one blessed, leads to the kingdom of heaven. And: Better to suffer injustice than to commit it, indeed, to bear insult and disgrace with Jesus instead of inflicting such things on others! Anyone who takes this path with Jesus already experiences joy now and will also experience "great reward in heaven" some day.

The "saints", whom the Church is celebrating today, the many well-known saints and the even greater number of hidden ones, of whom only God knows, are made of the "stuff" of these eight Beatitudes. Their good way is open to everyone, even to us.

List of Illustrations

Color plates:

I. Feofan Grek (Theophanes the Greek), icon: *The Transfiguration of Christ* (late fourteenth century), Moscow, Tretjakov Gallery.

II. Gospel Book of Otto III, *The Sermon on the Mount* (ca. 1000), Munich, Bayerische Staatsbibliothek.

III. Codex Egberti, *Jesus Walking on the Sea* (ca. 980), Trier, Staatsbibliothek.

IV. Michelangelo Merisi da Caravaggio, *The Calling of Saint Matthew* (1599/1600), Rome, S. Luigi dei Francesci.

V. Michelangelo Merisi da Caravaggio, *Doubting Thomas* (1600/1601), Potsdam, Foundation for Prussian Castles and Gardens, Berlin-Brandenburg.

VI. Michelangelo, *Pietà* (1499), overall view photographed by Robert Hupka (1965), Summit, N.J., Estate of Robert E. Hupka.

VII. Michelangelo, *Pietà* photographed by Robert Hupka, when the statue was being packed for transportation (1965), Summit, N.J., Estate of Robert E. Hupka.

VIII. Nicholas of Verdun, The Verdun Altar (1181), detail: *The Paschal Lamb* (Resurrection), Klosterneuburg, Stift Klosterneuburg.

Scripture Index